THE VICTORIA CROSS ROLL OF HONOUR

By the Same Author:

The Way to Glory – Men of the North-West who rode in The Charge of the Light Brigade.

Rorke's Drift – The Zulu War, 1879.

THE VICTORIA CROSS
ROLL OF HONOUR

James W. Bancroft

Published in 1989 by
AIM HIGH PRODUCTIONS
280 Liverpool Road,
Eccles, Manchester.
in association with
The Self Publishing Association Ltd.,
Lloyds Bank Chambers,
Upton-upon-Severn, Worcs.

A MEMBER OF

ISBN 1 85421 058 0

Cover designed by Karen Hill

Produced and Designed by The Self Publishing Association Ltd
Printed and Bound in Great Britain by Billing & Sons Ltd, Worcester

PREFACE

I originally prepared The Victoria Cross Roll Of Honour to fill a gap in my own militaria library, after discovering that no such reference work existed. It was later suggested to me that other students of the Victoria Cross would find the lists useful. After an encouraging response to some market research I decided to finance publication of the 'Roll' and make it available to fellow enthusiasts.

I consulted all the VC. citations in the London Gazette, then I researched further through the various military museums, and the publications listed in the bibliography. The recipients are arranged under the service, regiment, or corps, to which they belonged when they performed the deed that gained them the award. With references to those attached to other units. The names appear in chronological order, and each campaign is specified. I also thought it would be helpful to include a guide to how the old establishments have reorganised to form the modern army, and I have arranged the index, as far as possible, by separate campaigns. Many recipients gained other awards, but as this is specifically a VC Roll I have omitted them.

(P) indicates posthumous, the recipient having been killed in action before the award was officially gazetted. It must also be noted that many men gave their lives after receiving the medal and returning to the theatre of war.

In the year of the 50th anniversary of Britain's declaration of war with Hitler's Germany I dedicate this book to the men whose names appear in it, and to all those who have risked their lives in war so that I may remain free. With special thoughts for the glorious dead who never came home.

I would like to thank all the people who have assisted me in my research, and The Self Publishing Association Limited for their valuable help and guidance. As always, I must thank my dear wife and children for various reasons.

I claim no particular status for this book; I simply hope that fellow military enthusiasts find The Victoria Cross Roll Of Honour to be a useful addition to their bookshelves.

James W. Bancroft
Eccles 1989

CONTENTS

1. The Royal Navy, Royal Indian Marine, Royal Naval Reserve, and Royal Naval Volunteer Reserve.
2. The Royal Marine Artillery, Light Infantry and Commando.
3. The Royal Naval Air Service and The Fleet Air Arm.
4. The Royal Air Force (Formerly The Royal Flying Corps) and The Royal Air Force Volunteer Reserve.
5. 1st Royal Dragoons.
6. 1st King's Dragoon Guards.
7. 2nd Dragoon Guards (The Queen's Bays).
8. 2nd Dragoons (The Royal Scots Greys).
9. 4th Royal Irish Dragoon Guards.
10. 5th Dragoon Guards (Princess Charlotte of Wales's).
11. 6th Dragoons (The Inniskilling).
12. 7th Queen's Own Hussars.
13. 4th Queen's Own Light Dragoons (Later Hussars)
14. 8th King's Royal Irish Hussars.
15. 9th Queen's Royal Lancers.
16. 10th Royal Hussars (Prince of Wales's Own).
17. 11th Hussars (Prince Albert's Own).
18. 13th Light Dragoons (Later Hussars).
19. 18th Royal Hussars (Queen Mary's Own).
20. 14th King's Hussars.
21. 15th, The King's Hussars.
22. 19th Royal Hussars (Queen Alexandra's Own) (Formerly 1st Bengal European Light Cavalry).
23. 16th Queen's Lancers.
24. 5th Royal Irish Lancers.
25. 17th Lancers (Duke of Cambridge's Own).
26. 21st Lancers (Empress of India's).
27. The Machine-Gun Corps.
28. The Royal Tank Regiment (Formerly The Tank Corps).
29. The Indian Armoured Corps.
30. The Berkshire Yeomanry
31. 2nd Scottish Horse (Dragoons).
32. The North Irish Horse.
33. The Imperial Yeomanry (1st County of London).
34. The Royal Regiment of Artillery and Indian Artillery.
35. The Honourable Artillery Company.
36. The Corps of Royal Engineers and Indian Engineers.
37. Grenadier Guards.
38. Coldstream Guards.

39. Scots Guards (Formerly Scots Fusilier Guards).
40. Irish Guards.
41. Welsh Guards.
42. The Royal Scots (The Royal Regiment) (1st Foot).
43. The Queen's Royal Regiment (West Surrey) (2nd Foot).
44. The East Surrey Regiment (31st/70th Foot).
45. The Buffs (Royal East Kent) Regiment (3rd Foot).
46. The Royal West Kent Regiment (Queen's Own) (50th/97th Foot).
47. The Royal Sussex Regiment (35th/107th Foot).
48. The Middlesex Regiment (Duke of Cambridge's Own) (56th/77th Foot).
49. The King's Own (Royal Lancaster) Regiment (4th Foot).
50. The Border Regiment (34th/55th Foot).
51. The Royal Northumberland Fusiliers (5th Foot).
52. The Royal Warwickshire Regiment (Later Fusiliers) (6th Foot).
53. The Royal Fusiliers (City of London Regiment) (7th Foot).
54. The Lancashire Fusiliers (20th Foot).
55. The King's (Liverpool) Regiment (8th Foot).
56. The Manchester Regiment (63rd/96th Foot).
57. The Royal Norfolk Regiment (9th Foot).
58. The Suffolk Regiment (12th Foot).
59. The Royal Lincolnshire Regiment (10th Foot).
60. The Northamptonshire Regiment (48th/58th Foot).
61. The Bedfordshire and Hertfordshire Regiment (16th Foot).
62. The Essex Regiment (44th/55th Foot).
63. The Royal Leicestershire Regiment (17th Foot).
64. The Devonshire Regiment (11th Foot).
65. The Dorset Regiment (39th/54th Foot).
66. The Somerset Light Infantry (Prince Albert's)
67. The Duke of Cornwall's Light Infantry (32nd/46th Foot).
68. The King's Own Yorkshire Light Infantry (51st/105th Foot).
69. The King's Shropshire Light Infantry (53rd/85th Foot).
70. The Durham Light Infantry (68th/106th Foot).
71. The West Yorkshire Regiment (The Prince of Wales's Own) (14th Foot).
72. The East Yorkshire Regiment (Duke of York's Own) (15th Foot).
73. The Green Howards (Alexandra, Princess of Wales's Own Regiment of Yorkshire (19th Foot).
74. The Royal Scots Fusiliers (21st Foot).
75. The Highland Light Infantry (City of Glasgow Regiment) (71st/74th Highlanders).
76. The Cheshire Regiment (22nd Foot).
77. The Royal Welch Fusiliers (23rd Foot).
78. The South Wales Borderers and Monmouthshire Regiment (24th Foot).
79. The Welch Regiment (41st/69th Foot).
80. The King's Own Scottish Borderers (25th Foot).

81. The Cameronians (Scottish Rifles) (26th/90th Foot).

82. The Royal Inniskilling Fusiliers (27th/108th Foot).

83. The Royal Ulster Rifles (Formerly The Royal Irish Rifles) (83rd/86th Foot).

84. The Royal Irish Fusiliers (Princess Victoria's) (87th/89th Foot).

85. The Gloucestershire Regiment (28th/61st Foot).

86. The Worcestershire Regiment (29th/36th Foot).

87. The Sherwood Foresters (Nottinghamshire and Derbyshire Regiment) (45th/95th Foot).

88. The East Lancashire Regiment (30th/59th Foot).

89. The Prince of Wales's Volunteers (South Lancashire) Regiment (40th/82nd Foot).

90. The Loyal Regiment (North Lancashire) (47th/81st Foot).

91. The Duke of Wellington's Regiment (West Riding) (33rd/76th Foot).

92. The Royal Hampshire Regiment (37th/67th Foot).

93. The South Staffordshire Regiment (38th/80th Foot).

94. The North Staffordshire Regiment (The Prince of Wales's) (64th/98th Foot).

95. The Black Watch (The Royal Highland Regiment) (42nd/73rd Highlanders)

96. The Royal Berkshire Regiment (Princess Charlotte of Wales's) (49th/66th Foot).

97. The Wiltshire Regiment (Duke of Edinburgh's) (62nd/99th Foot).

98. The York and Lancaster Regiment (65th/84th Foot).

99. Seaforth Highlanders (Ross-Shire Buffs, The Duke of Albany's) (72nd/78th Highlanders).

100. Queen's Own Cameron Highlanders (79th Highlanders).

101. Gordon Highlanders (75th/92nd Highlanders).

102. Argyll and Sutherland Highlanders (Princess Louise's) (91st/93rd Highlanders).

103. The Parachute Regiment. (and Airborne Forces).

104. 2nd King Edward VII's Own Gurkha Rifles (The Sirmoor Rifles).

105. 3rd Queen Alexandra's Own Gurkha Rifles.

106. 5th Royal Gurkha Rifles.

107. 6th Queen Elizabeth's Own Gurkha Rifles.

108. 7th Duke of Edinburgh's Own Gurkha Rifles.

109. 8th Gurkha Rifles.

110. 9th Gurkha Rifles.

111. 10th Princess Mary's Own Gurkha Rifles.

112. The Oxfordshire and Buckinghamshire Light Infantry (43rd/52nd Foot).

113. The King's Royal Rifle Corps (60th Rifles).

114. The Rifle Brigade (Prince Consort's Own).

115. Special Forces.

116. The Royal Irish Regiment (18th Foot).

117. The Connaught Rangers (88th/94th Foot).

118. The Prince of Wales's Leinster Regiment (Royal Canadians) (100th/109th Foot).

119. The Royal Munster Fusiliers (101st/104th Foot).

120. The Royal Dublin Fusiliers (102nd/103rd Foot).
121. The London Regiment (Territorial Force).
122. The London Scottish Regiment (Territorial Force).
123. The Hertfordshire Regiment (Territorial Force).
124. The West India Regiment.
125. The Royal Army Chaplains' Department.
126. Military Train.
127. Commissariat and Transport Corps.
128. The Royal Army Service Corps.
129. The Army Hospital Corps.
130. The Army Medical Service.
131. The Royal Army Medical Corps.
132. The Indian Staff Corps. The Bengal Staff Corps, and The Bombay Staff Corps.
133. 1st Punjab Cavalry.
134. 2nd Punjab Cavalry.
135. 2nd Bombay Light Cavalry.
136. 3rd Bombay Light Cavalry.
137. 5th Bengal European Cavalry.
138. 6th Bengal European Cavalry.
139. 7th Hariana Lancers.
140. 14th Murray's Jat Horse (The Bengal Lancers).
141. 28th Light Cavalry.
142. 34th Prince Albert Victor's Own Poona Horse.
143. 1st Punjabi Regiment.
144. 2nd Bengal Native Infantry.
145. 4th Bengal European Regiment.
146. 4th Punjabi Infantry.
147. 4th Bengal Native Infantry.
148. 5th Mahratta Light Infantry.
149. 6th Rajputana Rifles.
150. 8th Punjabi Regiment.
151. 9th Bhopal Infantry.
152. 9th Jat Infantry.
153. 10th Baluchi Regiment.
154. 11th Bengal Native Infantry.
155. 11th Sikh Regiment.
156. 12th Frontier Force Rifles.
157. 13th Frontier Force Rifles.
158. 13th Bengal Native Infantry.
159. 15th Ludhiana Sikhs.
160. 15th Punjabi Regiment.
161. 16th Punjabi Regiment.
162. 19th Madras Native Infantry.
163. 20th Bombay Native Infantry.

164. 24th Bombay Native Infantry.
165. 25th Bombay Light Infantry.
166. 26th Bengal Native Infantry.
167. 28th Punjabi Regiment.
168. 37th Bengal Native Infantry.
169. 39th Garhwali Rifles.
170. 41st Dogras.
171. 46th Bengal Native Infantry.
172. 51st Sikhs (Frontier Force).
173. 55th Coke's Rifles (Frontier Force).
174. 56th Punjabi Rifles (Frontier Force).
175. 59th Scind Rifles.
176. 60th Bengal Native Infantry.
177. 66th Punjabis.
178. 72nd Punjabis.
179. 89th Punjabis.
180. 129th Duke of Connaught's Own Baluchis.
181. The Bengal Army (Unattached).
182. The Indian Medical Service.
183. The Indian Army Ordnance Department (Bengal Establishment).
184. Bengal Police Battalion.
185. The Bengal Veteran's Establishment.
186. The Bengal Ecclesiastical Establishment (Civilian).
187. The Bengal Civil Service.
188. The South African Air Force.
189. The Frontier Light Horse.
190. The Natal Native Contingent.
191. The Cape Mounted Rifles
192. The Cape Mounted Yeomanry (1st Regiment).
193. Nourse's Transvaal Horse.
194. Mashonaland Mounted Police.
195. The Bulawayo Field Force.
196. The Protectorate Regiment (North West Cape Colony).
197. Rimington's Guides.
198. The Cape Police.
199. The South African Constabulary.
200. The Imperial Light Horse (Natal).
201. Scout's Corps (2nd South African Mounted Brigade).
202. The South African Light Infantry.
203. The British South African Police.
204. The King's African Rifles.
205. The Royal Natal Carbineers.
206. The Kaffiarian Rifles.
207. The Royal Canadian Naval Volunteer Reserve.

208. The Royal Canadian Air Force.
209. Royal Canadian Dragoons.
210. Lord Strathcona's Corps (Canadian Cavalry).
211. The Fort Garry Horse (Canadian Cavalry).
212. The Canadian Machine-Gun Corps.
213. The Canadian Armoured Corps.
214. Canadian Engineers.
215. Canadian Mounted Rifles (Infantry).
216. Canadian Infantry Corps.
217. The Canadian Chaplains' Service.
218. The Canadian Army Medical Service.
219. The Royal Newfoundland Regiment.
220. The Royal Australian Air Force (Australian Flying Corps).
221. 5th Australian Field Artillery.
222. Tasmanian Imperial Bushmen.
223. The New South Wales Medical Staff Corps.
224. West Australian Mounted Infantry.
225. 5th Victorian Mounted Rifles.
226. 10th Australian Light Horse.
227. The Australian Machine-Gun Corps.
228. The Australian Infantry Corps.
229. The Australian Army Training Team.
230. The Royal New Zealand Air Force.
231. The Auckland Militia.
232. 4th New Zealand Contingent.
233. New Zealand Engineers.
234. The New Zealand Infantry Corps.
235. Fijian Infantry.
236. The Unknown Warrior of the United States of America.

1. THE ROYAL NAVY, ROYAL INDIAN MARINE, ROYAL NAVAL RESERVE, AND ROYAL NAVAL VOLUNTEER RESERVE

Crimea

Mate Charles Davis Lucas, HMS *Hecla;* 1854 – The Baltic

Lieutenant John Bythesea, HMS *Arrogant;* 1854 – The Baltic

Stoker William Johnstone, HMS *Arrogant*; 1854 – The Baltic

Captain William Peel, *Naval Brigade;* 1854-55 – Inkerman & Sebastopol

Lieutenant William Nathan Wrighte Hewett, *Naval Brigade;* 1854 – Inkerman

Midshipman Edward St John Daniel, *Naval Brigade;* 1854-55 – Inkerman & Sebastopol

Seaman James Gorman, *Naval Brigade;* 1854 - Inkerman

Seaman Thomas Reeves, *Naval Brigade;* 1854 – Inkerman

Seaman Mark Scholefield, *Naval Brigade;* 1854 – Inkerman

Botswain's Mate John Sullivan, *Naval Brigade;* 1855 – Sebastopol

Lieutenant Cecil William Buckley, HMS *Miranda;* 1855 – Sea of Azov

Lieutenant Hugh Talbot Burgoyne, HMS *Swallow;* 1855 – Sea of Azov

Gunner John Robarts, HMS *Ardent;* 1855 – Sea of Azov

Botswain Henry Cooper, HMS *Miranda;* 1855 – Sea of Azov

Commander Henry James Raby, *Naval Brigade;* 1855 – Sebastopol

Captain of The Forecastle John Taylor, *Naval Brigade;* 1855 – Sebastopol

Botswain's Mate Henry Curtis, *Naval Brigade;* 1855 – Sebastopol

Seaman Joseph Trewavas, HMS *Beagle;* 1855 – Sea of Azov

Captain of The Mast George Henry Ingouville, HMS *Arrogant;* 1855 – The Baltic

Botswain John Sheppard, *Naval Brigade;* 1855 – Sebastopol

Botswain Joseph Kellaway, HMS *Wrangler;* 1855 – Marionpol

Commander George Fiott Day, HMS *Recruit; 1855* – Sea of Azov

Commander John Edmund Commerell, HMS *Weser; 1855* – Sea of Azov

Quartermaster William Thomas Rickard, HMS *Weser; 1855* – Sea of Azov

Indian Mutiny

Lieutenant Nowell Salmon, *Naval Brigade;* 1857 – Lucknow

Botswain's Mate John Harrison, *Naval Brigade;* 1857 – Lucknow

Lieutenant Thomas James Young, *Naval Brigade;* 1857 – Lucknow

Able Seaman William Hall, *Naval Brigade;* 1857 – Lucknow

Midshipman Arthur Mayo, *Naval Brigade;* 1857 – Dacca

Seaman Edward Robinson, Naval Brigade; 1858 – Lucknow

Volunteer George Bell Chicken, Naval Brigade; 1858 – Suhejnee

New Zealand

Leading Seaman William Odgers, HMS *Niger;* 1860 – Waireka

China

Able Seaman George Hinckley, HMS *Sphinx;* 1862 – Shanghai

New Zealand

Captain of The Foretop Samuel Mitchell, HMS *Harrier;* 1864 – Tauranga

Japan

Midshipman Duncan Gordon Boyes, HMS *Euryalus;* 1864 – Straits of Simona Seki

Captain of The After Guard Thomas Pride, HMS *Euryalus;* 1864 – Straits of Simono Seki

Seaman William Henry Harrison Seeley, HMS *Euryalus;* 1864 – Straits of Simono Seki

Egypt

Gunner Israel Harding, HMS *Alexandra;* 1882 - Alexandria

Sudan

Captain Arthur Knyvet Wilson, *Naval Brigade;* 1884 – El Teb

Crete

Surgeon William Job Maillard, HMS *Hazzard;* 1898 – Candia

China

Midshipman Basil John Douglas Guy, HMS *Barfleur;* 1900 – Tientsin

The Great War

Commander Henry Peel Ritchie, HMS *Goliath;* 1914 – Dar-es-Salaam

Lieutenant Norman Douglas Holbrook, HMS/MB 11; 1914 – Dardanelles

Lieutenant-Commander Eric Gascoigne Robinson, HMS *Vengeance;* 1915 – Dardanelles

Commander Edward Unwin, HMS *River Clyde;* 1915 – Gallipoli

Midshipman RNR George Leslie Drewry, HMS *River Clyde;* 1915 – Gallipoli

Midshipman Wilfred St Aubyn Malleson, HMS *River Clyde;* 1915 – Gallipoli

(P) Able Seaman William Charles Williams, HMS *River Clyde;* 1915 – Gallipoli

Seaman RNR George McKenzie Samson, HMS *River Clyde;* 1915 – Gallipoli

(P) Sub-Lieutenant RNVR Arthur Walderne St Clair Tisdall, Anson Battalion, RN Division; 1915 – Gallipoli

Lieutenant-Commander Edward Courtney Boyle, HMS/ME 14; 1915 – Dardanelles

Lieutenant-Commander Martin Eric Nasmith, HMS/ME 11; 1915 – Dardanelles

(P) Lieutenant RNR Frederick Daniel Parslow, HMT *Anglo Californian;* 1915 – Atlantic

(P) Lieutenant-Commander Edgar Christopher Cookson, HMS *Comet;* 1915 – Kut-el-Amara

(P) Lieutenant Humphrey Osbaldeston Brooke Firman, SS *Julnar;* 1915 – Kut-el-Amara

(P) Lieutenant-Commander RNVR Charles Henry Cowley, SS *Julnar;* 1915 – Kut-el-Amara

Commander Edward Barry Stewart Bingham, HMS *Nestor;* 1916 – Jutland

(P) Boy 1st Class John Travers Cornwell, HMS *Chester;* 1916 – Jutland

(P) Commander Loftus William Jones, HMS *Shark;* 1916 – Jutland

Commander Gordon Campbell, HMS *Q5;* 1917 – Atlantic

(P) Lieutenant RNR Archibald Bisset Smith, SS *Otaki;* 1917 – Atlantic

Lieutenant RNR William Edward Sanders, HMS *Prize;* 1917 – Atlantic

Lieutenant RNR Ronald Niel Stuart, HMS *Pargust;* 1917 – Atlantic

Seaman RNR William Williams, HMS *Pargust;* 1917 – Atlantic

Lieutenant RNR Charles George Bonner, HMS *Dunraven;* 1917 – Atlantic

Petty Officer Ernest Herbert Pitcher, HMS *Dunraven;* 1917 – Atlantic

Skipper RNR Joseph Watt, HM Drifter *Gowan Lea;* 1917 – Otranto Straits

(P) Skipper RNR Thomas Crisp, HM Smack *Nelson;* 1917 – North Sea

(P) Ordinary Seaman John Henry Carless, HMS *Caledon;* 1917 – Heligoland

(P) Lieutenant-Commander Geoffrey Saxton White, HMS/ME 14; 1918 – Dardanelles

Commander Alfred Francis Blakeney Carpenter, HMS *Vindictive;* 1918 – Zeebrugge

Lieutenant-Commander Arthur Leyland Harrison, HMS *Vindictive;* 1918 – Zeebrugge

Able Seaman Albert Edward McKenzie, HMS *Vindictive;* 1918 – Zeebrugge

(P) Lieutenant-Commander George Nicholson Bradford, HMS *Iris II;* 1918 – Zeebrugge

Lieutenant Richard Douglas Sandford, HMS/MC 3; 1918 – Zeebrugge

Lieutenant RNVR Percy Thompson Dean, HM Motor Launch 254; 1918 – Zeebrugge

Lieutenant Victor Alexander Charles Crutchley, HMS *Vindictive;* 1918 – Ostend

Lieutenant-Commander RNVR Geoffrey Heneage Drummond, HM Motor Launch 254; 1918 – Ostend

Lieutenant-Commander RNVR Roland Richard Louis Bourke, HM Motor Launch 276; 1918 – Ostend

Lieutenant RNR Harold Auten, HMS *Stock Force;* 1918 – English Channel

Commander RNVR Daniel Marcus William Beak, Drake Battalion, RN Division; 1918 – France

(P) Chief Petty-Officer RNVR George Prowse, Drake Battalion, RN Division; 1918 – France

Lieutenant Augustine Willington Shelton Agar, HM CMB 4; 1919 – Kronstadt

Commander Claude Congreve Dobson, HM CMB 31; 1919 – Kronstadt

Lieutenant Gordon Charles Steele, HM CMB 88; 1919 – Kronstadt

2nd World War

(P) Lieutenant-Commander Gerard Broadmead Roope, HMS *Glowworm;* 1940 – Norwegian Sea

(P) Captain Bernard Armitage Warburton Warburton-Lee, HMS *Hardy;* 1940 – Narvik

Lieutenant RNR Richard Been Stannard, HMS *Arab;* 1940 – Namsos

(P) Leading Seaman Jack Foreman Mantle, HMS *Foylebank;* 1940 – Portland

(P) Captain Edward Stephen Fogarty Fegen, HMS *Jervis Bay;* 1940 – Atlantic

Petty Officer Alfred Edward Sephton, HMS *Coventry;* 1941 – Crete

Lieutenant-Commander Malcolm David Wanklyn, HMS/M *Upholder;* 1941 – Mediterranean

(P) Lieutenant RNR Thomas Wilkinson, HMS *Li Wo;* 1942 – Java Sea

Lieutenant Peter Scawen Watkinson Roberts, HMS/M *Thrasher;* 1942 – Mediterranean

Petty Officer Thomas William Gould, HMS/M *Thrasher;* 1942 – Mediterranean

Commander Anthony Cecil Capel Miers, HMS/M *Torbay;* 1942 – Corfu Roads

Commander Robert Edward Dudley Rider, HM MGB 314; 1942 – St Nazaire

Lieutenant-Commander Stephen Halden Beattie, HMS *Campbeltown;* 1942 – St Nazaire

(P) Able Seaman William Alfred Savage, HM MGB 314; 1942 – St Nazaire

(P) Captain Frederick Thornton Peters, HMS *Walney;* 1942 – Oran Harbour

Captain Robert St Vincent Sherbrooke, HMS *Onslow;* 1942 – Barents Sea

(P) Commander John Wallace Linton, HMS/M *Turbulent;* 1943 – Mediterranean

Lieutenant RNR Donald Cameron, HMS/MX 7; 1943 – Kaafjord

Lieutenant Basil Charles Godfrey Place, HMS/MX 6; 1943 – Kaafjord

Lieutenant Ian Edward Fraser, HMS/MXE 3; 1945 – Johore Straits

Leading Seaman James Joseph Magennis, HMS/MXE 3; 1945 – Johore Straits

See also: 43

2. THE ROYAL MARINE ARTILLERY, LIGHT INFANTRY and COMMANDO

Crimea

Corporal John Prettyjohn, RMLI: 1854 – Inkerman

Bombardier Thomas Wilkinson, RMA: 1854 – Sebastopol

Lieutenant George Dare Dowell, RMA: 1855 – The Baltic

China

Captain Lewis Stratford Tollemache Halliday, RMLI: 1900 – Pekin

The Great War

Lance-Corporal Walter Richard Parker, RMLI: 1915 – Gallipoli

(P) Major Francis John William Harvey, RMLI: *HMS Lion;* 1916 – Jutland

Major Frederick William Lumsden, RMA: 1917 – France

(P) Captain Edward Bamford, RMLI: 1918 – Zeebrugge:

Sergeant Norman Augustus Finch, RMA: *HMS Vindictive:* 1918 – Zeebrugge

2nd World War

(P) Corporal Thomas Peck Hunter, 43 Commando: 1945 – Italy

See also: 131.

3. THE ROYAL NAVAL AIR SERVICE and THE FLEET AIR ARM

The Great War

Flight Sub-Lieutenant Reginald Alexander John Warneford, No 1 Squadron, RNAS: 1915 – Belgium

Squadron-Commander Richard Bell Davies, No 3 Squadron, RNAS: 1915 – Bulgaria

2nd World War

(P) Lieutenant-Commander Eugene Esmonde, No 825 Squadron, FAA: 1942 – Dover Straits

See also: 207

4. THE ROYAL AIR FORCE
(Formerly THE ROYAL FLYING CORPS) and THE ROYAL AIR FORCE VOLUNTEER RESERVE

(P) 2nd Lieutenant William Barnard Rhodes-Moorehouse, (Special Reserve); No 2 Squadron RFC; 1915 – Belgium

2nd Lieutenant Gilbert Stuart Martin Insall, No 11 Squadron, RFC: 1917 – Belgium

(P) Sergeant Thomas Mottershead, No 20 Squadron, RFC: 1917 – Belgium

Captain James Thomas Byford McCudden, General List – No 56 Squadron, RFC: 1917-18 – France

(P) Lieutenant Alan Jerrard, No 66 Squadron, RFC: 1918 – Italy
(Formerly with The South Staffordshire Regiment)

(P) 2nd Lieutenant Alan Arnett McCleod, No 2 Squadron, RFC: 1918 – France

Captain Ferdinand Maurice Felix West, No 8 Squadron, RFC: 1918 – France
(Formerly Special Reserve, The Royal Munster Fusiliers)

Act. Major William George Barker, No 201 Squadron, RFC: 1918 – France

Act. Captain Andrew Frederick Weatherby Beauchamp-Proctor, No 84 Squadron, RFC: 1918 – France

(P) Major Edward Mannock, No 85 Squadron, RFC: 1918 – France

2nd World War

(P) Flying Officer Donald Edward Garland, No 12 Squadron, RAF: 1940 – Belgium

(P) Sergeant Thomas Gray, No 12 Squadron, RAF: 1940 – Belgium

Flight-Lieutenant Roderick Alastair Brook Learoyd, No 49 Squadron, RAF: 1940 – Germany

Flight-Lieutenant Eric James Brindley Nicolson, No 249 Squadron, RAF: 1940 – England

Sergeant John Hannah, No 83 Squadron, RAF: 1940 – Belgium

(P) Flying Officer Kenneth Campbell, No 22 Squadron RAFVR, (Coastal Command) 1941 – France

Wing-Commander Hughie Idwal Edwards, No 105 Squadron, RAF: 1941 – Germany

Squadron-Leader Arthur Stuart King Scarf, No 62 Squadron, RAF: 1941 – Thailand

Squadron-Leader John Dering Nettleton, No 44 Squadron, RAF: 1942 – Germany

Flying Officer Leslie Thomas Manser, No 50 Squadron, RAFVR: 1942 – Germany

(P) Wing-Commander Hugh Gordon Malcolm, No 18 Squadron, RAF: 1942 – North Africa

Wing-Commander Guy Penrose Gibson, No 617 Squadron, RAF: 1943 – Germany

(P) Act. Flight-Sergeant Arthur Louis Aaron, No 218 Squadron, RAFVR: 1943 – Italy

Act. Flight-Lieutenant William Reid, No 61 Squadron, RAFVR: 1943 – Germany

Pilot-Officer Cyril Joseph Barton, No 578 Squadron, RAFVR: 1944 – Germany

Sergeant Norman Cyril Jackson, No 106 Squadron, RAFVR: 1944 – Germany

Flying-Officer John Alexander Cruickshank, No 210 Squadron, RAFVR: (Coastal Command): 1944 – Norway

Act. Squadron-Leader Ian Willoughby Bazalgette, No 635 Squadron, RAFVR: 1944 – France

Flight-Lieutentant David Samuel Anthony Lord, No 217 Squadron, (Transport Command, Airborne Forces) 1944 – Holland

Squadron Leader Robert Anthony Maurice Palmer, No 109 Squadron, RAFVR: 1944 – Germany

Wing Commander Geoffrey Leonard Cheshire, RAFVR: 1940-44 6 Flying Operations

(P) Flight-Sergeant George Thompson, No 9 Squadron, RAFVR: 1945 – Germany

See also: 86 87 188 215 220 230

5. 1st ROYAL DRAGOONS

The Great War

(P) 2nd Lieutenant John Spencer Dunville: 1917 – France

6. 1st KING'S DRAGOON GUARDS

Transvaal (Boer)

Private John Doogan, 1881 – Laing's Nek

7. 2nd DRAGOON GUARDS (THE QUEEN'S BAYS)

Indian Mutiny

Lieutenant Robert Blair, 1857 – Bolundshahur

Corporal Charles Anderson, 1858 – Lucknow

Trumpeter Thomas Monaghan: 1858 – Lucknow

Sudan

Captain Nevill Maskelyne Smyth: 1898 – Khartoum

8.   2nd DRAGOONS
(THE ROYAL SCOTS GREYS)

Crimea

Sergeant-Major John Grieve: 1854 – Balaclava
Sergeant Henry Ramage: 1854 – Balaclava

2nd World War

(P) Major Geoffrey Charles Tasker Keyes: 1941 – Western Desert

9.   4th ROYAL IRISH DRAGOON GUARDS

The Great War

Captain Adrian Carton de Wiart: 1916 – France
(Attached: 8th Btn. The Gloucestershire Regiment)

10.   5th DRAGOON GUARDS
(PRINCESS CHARLOTTE OF WALES'S)

South Africa (Boer)

2nd Lieutenant John Norwood: 1899 – Ladysmith

11.   6th DRAGOONS
(THE INNISKILLING)

Crimea

Surgeon James Mouat: 1854 – Balaclava

12.   7th QUEEN'S OWN HUSSARS

Indian Mutiny

(P) Cornet William George Hawtrey Bankes: 1858 – Lucknow
Major Charles Craufurd Fraser: 1858 – Lucknow

13. 4th QUEEN'S OWN LIGHT DRAGOONS (Later HUSSARS)

Crimea

Private Samuel Parkes: 1854 – Balaclava

14. 8th KING'S ROYAL IRISH HUSSARS

Indian Mutiny

Captain Clement Walker Heneage: 1858 – Gwalior

Sergeant Joseph Ward: 1858 – Gwalior

Farrier George Hollis: 1858 – Gwalior

Private John Pearson: 1858 – Gwalior

Troop Sergeant-Major James Champion: 1858 – Central India

15. 9th QUEEN'S ROYAL LANCERS

Indian Mutiny

Lieutenant Alfred Stowell Jones: 1857 – Delhi

Sergeant Henry Hartigan: 1857 – Delhi

Private Thomas Hancock: 1857 – Budle-ke-Serai

Private John Purcell: 1857 – Budle-ke-Serai

Lance-Corporal Robert Kells: 1857 – Bolundshahur

Private Patrick Donohoe: 1857 – Bolundshahur

Private James Reynolds Roberts: 1857 – Bolundshahur

Private John Freeman: 1857 – Agra

Troop Sergeant-Major David Spence: 1858 – Lucknow

Lance-Corporal William Goat: 1858 – Lucknow

Troop Sergeant-Major David Rushe: 1858 – Lucknow

Private Robert Newell: 1858 – Lucknow

The Zulu War

Captain, The Lord William Leslie de la Poer Beresford: 1879 – Ulundi

The Great War

Captain Francis Octavius Grenfell: 1914 – Belgium

16.   10th ROYAL HUSSARS
(PRINCE OF WALES'S OWN)

South Africa (Boer)

Lieutenant, Sir John Penistone Milbanke: 1900 – Colesberg

Sergeant Henry William Engleheart: 1900 – Bloemfontein

17.   11th HUSSARS
(PRINCE ALBERT'S OWN)

Crimea

Lieutenant Alexander Roberts Dunn: 1854 – Balaclava

18.   13th LIGHT DRAGOONS
(Later HUSSARS)

Crimea

Corporal Joseph Malone: 1854 – Balaclava

19.   18th ROYAL HUSSARS
(QUEEN MARY'S OWN)

South Africa (Boer)

Private Henry George Crandon: 1901 – Transvaal

20.   14th KING'S HUSSARS

Indian Mutiny

Lieutenant James Leith: 1858 – Jhansi

South Africa (Boer)

Major Edward Douglas Brown: 1900 – Geluk Farm
(Later Brown-Synge-Hutchinson)

21.   15th THE KING'S HUSSARS

The Great War

Corporal Charles Ernest Garforth: 1914 – Belgium

22. 19th ROYAL HUSSARS (QUEEN ALEXANDRA'S OWN) (Formerly 1st BENGAL EUROPEAN LIGHT CAVALRY)

Indian Mutiny

Lieutenant Hugh Henry Gough: 1857 – Lucknow

Sudan

Quartermaster-Sergeant William Marshall: 1884 – El Teb

23. 16th QUEEN'S LANCERS

North West Frontier, India

Lieutenant, Viscount Alexander Edward Murray Fincastle: 1897 – Upper Swat

24. 5th ROYAL IRISH LANCERS

South Africa (Boer)

Lieutenant Frederick Brooks Dugdale: 1901 – Derby

The Great War

(P) Private George William Clare: 1917 – France

25. 17TH LANCERS (DUKE OF CAMBRIDGE'S OWN)

Crimea

Troop Sergeant-Major John Berryman: 1854 – Balaclava
Quartermaster-Sergeant John Farrell: 1854 – Balaclava
Sergeant-Major Charles Wooden: 1854 – Balaclava

Indian Mutiny

Lieutenant Henry Evelyn Wood: 1858 – Central India

South Africa (Boer)

Sergeant Brian Turner Lawrence: 1900 – Essenbosch Farm

26. 21st LANCERS
(EMPRESS OF INDIA'S)

Sudan

Captain Paul Aloysius Kenna: 1898 – Omdurman

Lieutenant, The Hon. Raymond Harvey Lodge Joseph De Montmorency: 1898 – Omdurman

Private Thomas Byrne: 1898 – Omdurman

The Great War

Private (Shoeing-Smith) Charles Hull: 1915 – India

27. THE MACHINE-GUN CORPS

The Great War

Lance-Corporal Harold Sandford Mugford, 8th Squadron: 1917 – France

(P) Private Herbert George Columbine, 9th Squadron: 1918 – France

Private Arthur Henry Cross, 40th Squadron: 1918 – France
(Formerly served with the 21st London Regiment)

Temp. 2nd Lieutenant William Allison White, 38th Squadron: 1918 – France

See also: 42 101 102

28. THE ROYAL TANK REGIMENT
(Formerly THE TANK CORPS)

The Great War

(P) Temp. Lieutenant Richard William Leslie Wain, 1st Btn: 1917 – France

2nd World War

Act. Captain Philip John Gardner, 4th Btn, 1941 – Libya

Temp. Lieutenant-Colonel Henry Robert Bowreman Foote, Commanding 7th Btn, 1942 – Libya

See also: 32 43 46

29. THE INDIAN ARMOURED CORPS

2nd World War

(P) Act. Captain Michael Allmand: 1944 – Burma
(Attached: 6th Queen Elizabeth's Own Gurkha Rifles)

30. THE BERKSHIRE YEOMANRY

The Great War

Private Frederick William Owen Potts, 1/1st: Btn. 1915 – Gallipoli

31. 2nd SCOTTISH HORSE (DRAGOONS)

South Africa (Boer)

Lieutenant William John English: 1901 – Vlakfontein

32. THE NORTH IRISH HORSE

The Great War

(P) Act. Lieutenant-Colonel Richard Annesley West: Special Reserve: 1918 – France
(Attached: 6th Btn. The Tank Corps)

33. THE IMPERIAL YEOMANRY
(1st COUNTY OF LONDON)

South Africa (Boer)

Lieutenant Alexis Charles Doxat, 3rd Btn: 1900 – Transvaal

The Great War

(P) Major Alexander Malins Lafone, 2/1st; Btn. 1917 – Palestine

34. THE ROYAL REGIMENT OF ARTILLERY
AND INDIAN ARTILLERY

Crimea

Colonel Collingwood Dickson: 1854 – Sebastapol

Major Frederick Miller: 1854 – Inkerman

Captain Andrew Henry: 1854 – Inkerman

Captain Matthew Charles Dixon: 1855 – Sebastopol

Sergeant George Symons: 1854 – Sebastopol
(Later served as Lieutenant, Military Train)

Gunner and Driver Thomas Arthur: 1855 – Sebastopol

Captain Gronow Davis: 1855 – Sebastopol

Bombardier Daniel Cambridge: 1855 – Sebastopol

Lieutenant Christopher Charles Teesdale: 1855 – Kars

Indian Mutiny

Gunner William Connolly, Bengal Artillery: 1857 – Punjab

Lieutenant-Colonel Henry Tombs, Bengal Artillery: 1857 – Delhi

2nd Lieutenant James Hills, Bengal Artillery: 1857 – Delhi

Captain George Alexander Renny, Bengal Artillery: 1857 – Delhi

Captain Francis Cornwallis Maude, Bengal Artillery: 1857 – Lucknow

Captain William Olpherts, Bengal Artillery: 1857 – Lucknow

Bombardier Jacob Thomas, Bengal Artillery: 1857 – Lucknow

Sergeant Bernard Diamond, Bengal Artillery: 1857 – Bolundshahur

Gunner Richard Fitzgerald, Bengal Artillery: 1857 – Bolundshahur

Lieutenant Hastings Edward Harington, Bengal Artillery: 1857 – Lucknow

Rough-Rider Edward Jennings, Bengal Artillery: 1857 – Lucknow

Gunner Thomas Laughnan, Bengal Artillery: 1857 – Lucknow

Gunner Hugh McInnes, Bengal Artillery: 1857 – Lucknow

Gunner James Park, Bengal Artillery: 1857 – Lucknow

Lieutenant Frederick Sleigh Roberts, Bengal Artillery: 1858 – Oudh

Major Richard Harte Keatinge, Bengal Artillery: 1858 – Central India

Bombardier Joseph Brennan, Bengal Artillery: 1858 – Jhansi

New Zealand

Assistant Surgeon William Temple: 1863 – Rangiriri

Lieutenant Arthur Frederick Pickard: 1863 – Rangiriri

Assistant Surgeon William George Nicholas Manley: 1864 – Tauranga

Afghanistan

Sergeant Patrick Mullane: 1880 – Maiwand

Gunner James Collis: 1880 – Maiwand

Sudan

Gunner Alfred Smith: 1885 – Abu Klea

South Africa (Boer)

Captain Harold Norton Schofield: 1899 – Colenso

Captain Hamilton Lyster Reed, 7th Btty: 1899 – Colenso

Corporal George Edward Nurse, 66th Btty: 1899 – Colenso

Major Edmund John Phipps-Hornby, Q Btty: 1900 – Korn Spruit

Sergeant Charles Edward Haydon Parker, Q Btty: 1900 – Korn Spruit

Gunner Isaac Lodge, Q Btty: 1900 – Korn Spruit

Driver Horace Henry Glasock, Q Btty: 1900 – Korn Spruit

Driver Frederick Henry Bradley, 69th Btty: 1901 – Zululand

Shoeing-Smith Alfred Ernest Ind, 11th Pom Pom: 1901 – Orange Free State

The Great War

Lieutenant-Colonel Ernest Wright Alexander, 119th Btty: 1914 – France

Captain Douglas Reynolds, 37th Btty: 1914 – France

Driver Job Henry Charles Drain, 37th Btty: 1914 – France

Driver Frederick Luke, 37th Btty: 37th Btty: 1914 – France

(P) Captain Edward Kinder Bradbury, L Btty: 1914 – France

Battery-Sergeant-Major George Thomas Dorrell, L Btty: 1914 – France

Sergeant David Nelson, L Btty: 1914 – France

Bombardier Ernest George Horlock, 113th Btty: 1914 – France

(P) Captain Garth Nevill Walford: 1915 – Gallipoli
(Brigade-Major, Mediterranean Expeditionary Force)

Act. Sergeant John Crawshaw Raynes, A/71st Btty: 1915 – France

Captain Lionel Wilmot Brabazon Rees: 1916 – France
(Serving with 32 Squadron, Royal Flying Corps)

Sergeant William Gosling, 3rd Wessex Brigade: 1917 – France

2nd Lieutenant Thomas Harold Broadbent Maufe, 124th Seige Btty: 1917 – France

Temp. Lieutenant Samuel Thomas Dickson Wallace, C/63rd Brigade: 1917 – France

Sergeant Cyril Edward Gourley, D/276th Brigade: 1917 – France

Gunner Charles Edwin Stone, C/83rd Brigade: 1918 – France

(P) Lieutenant Eric Stuart Dougall, Special Reserve: 1918 – Belgium
(Attached: C/88th Brigade)

Temp. Lieutenant Robert Vaughan Gorle, A/50th Btty: 1918 – France

2nd World War

Act. Brigadier John Charles Campbell: 1941 – Tobruk
(Commanding 7th Armoured Division)

(P) 2nd Lieutenant George Ward Gunn, 3rd Btty: 1941 – Tobruk

Temp. Captain Patrick Anthony Porteous: 1942 – France

Havildar Umrao Singh, Royal Indian Artillery: 1944 – Burma

See also: 82 131

35. THE HONOURABLE ARTILLERY COMPANY

The Great War

2nd Lieutenant Reginald Leonard Haine, 1st Btty: 1917 – France

2nd Lieutenant Alfred Oliver Pollard, 1st Btty: 1917 – France

36. THE CORPS OF ROYAL ENGINEERS And INDIAN ENGINEERS

Crimea

Lieutenant Wilbraham Oates Lennox: 1854 – Sebastopol

Corporal William James Lendrim: 1854 – Sebastopol

Colour-Sergeant Henry McDonald: 1854 – Sebastopol

Captain Howard Crawfurd Elphinstone: 1854 – Sebastopol

Lieutenant Gerald Graham: 1855 – Sebastopol

Colour-Sergeant Peter Leitch: 1855 – Sebastopol

Sapper John Perie: 1855 – Sebastopol

Corporal John Ross: 1855 – Sebastopol

Indian Mutiny

Lieutenant Duncan Charles Home, Bengal Engineers: 1857 – Delhi

Lieutenant Philip Salkeld, Bengal Engineers: 1857 – Delhi

Sergeant John Smith, Bengal Sappers & Miners: 1857 – Delhi

Lieutenant Edward Talbot Thackeray, Bengal Engineers: 1857 – Delhi

Lieutenant Henry North Dalrymple Prendergast, Madras Engineers: 1857 – Central India

Lieutenant John James McLeod Innes, Bengal Engineers: 1857 – Sultanpore

Corporal Michael Sleavon: 1858 – Jhansi

Lieutenant Charles Augustus Goodfellow: Bombay Engineers: 1858 – Central India

India

Major William Spottiswoode Trevor: 1865 – Bhootan
Lieutenant James Dundas: 1865 – Bhootan

Ashanti

Lieutenant Mark Sever Bell: 1874 – Ordalsu

The Zulu War

Lieutenant John Rouse Merriott Chard: 1879 – Rorke's Drift

Afghanistan

Lieutenant Reginald Clare Hart: 1879 – Peshawar
Captain Edward Pemberton Leach: 1879 – Maidanhah

North West Frontier, India

Captain Fenton John Aylmer: 1891 – Hunza

North West Frontier, India

Lieutenant James Morris Colquhoun Colvin: 1897 – Tirah
Lieutenant James Colclough Watson: 1897 – Tirah

South Africa (Boer)

Lieutenant Robert James Thomas Digby Jones: 1900 – Ladysmith
Corporal Frank Howard Kirby: 1900 – Delagoa Bay

The Great War

(P) Captain Theodore Wright, 57th Company: 1914 – Belgium
Lance-Corporal Charles Alfred Jarvis, 57th Company: 1914 – Belgium
Captain William Henry Johnston, 59th Company: 1914 – France
Lieutenant Philip Neame, 15th Company: 1914 – France
Lieutenant Cyril Gordon Martin, 56th Company: 1915 – Belgium
Captain Lance George Hawker: 1915 – France
(Serving with 6th Squadron, Royal Flying Corps)

Temp. 2nd Lieutenant Frederick Henry Johnson, 73rd Company: 1915 – France

Corporal James Lennox Dawson, 187th Company: 1915 – France

(P) Sapper William Hackett, 254th Tunnelling Company: 1916 – France

Lieutenant-Colonel Clifford Coffin: 1917 – Belgium
(Commanding 25th Infantry Brigade)

(P) Corporal James McPhie, 416th Company: 1918 – France

Captain George de Cardonne Elmsall Findlay, 409th Company: 1918 – France

Act. Major Brett Mackay Cloutman, 59th Company: 1918 – France

Temp. 2nd Lieutenant Cecil Leonard Knox, 150th Company: 1918 – France

(P) Sapper Adam Archibald, 218th Company: 1918 – France

(P) Temp. Captain Arnold Horace Santo Waters, 218th Company: 1918 – France

2nd World War

2nd Lieutenant Premindra Singh Bhagat, Indian Engineers: 1914 – Abyssinia
(Attached: Royal Bombay Sappers & Miners)

(P) Sergeant Thomas Frank Durrant: 1942 – France
(HM MGB 306, Attached: No 1 Commando Unit)

(P) Lieutenant Claud Raymond: 1945 – Burma

37. GRENADIER GUARDS

Crimea

Colonel, The Hon. Henry Hugh Manvers Percy, 3rd Btn: 1854 – Inkerman

Brevet-Major, Sir Charles Russell, 3rd Btn: 1854 – Inkerman

Private Anthony Palmer, 3rd Btn: 1854 – Inkerman

Sergeant Alfred Ablett, 3rd Btn: 1855 – Sabastopol

The Great War

Lance-Corporal Wilfred Dolby Fuller, 1st Btn: 1915 – France

(P) Private Edward Barber, 1st Btn: 1915 – France

(P) Lance-Sergeant John Harold Rhodes, 3rd Btn: 1917 – Belgium

(P) Act. Captain George Henry Tathan Paton, 4th Btn: 1917 – France

(P) Act. Captain Thomas Tannant Pryce, 4th Btn: 1918 – France

Act. Lieutenant-Colonel, Viscount John Standish Surtees Prendergast Vereker Gort, 1st Btn: 1918 – France

(P) Private William Edgar Holmes, 2nd Btn: 1918 – France

2nd World War

Lance-Corporal Henry Nicholls, 3rd Btn: 1940 – Belgium

Temp. Major William Philip Sidney, 5th Btn: 1944 – Italy
(later The Viscount De L'isle)

See also: 216

38. COLDSTREAM GUARDS

Crimea

Private William Stanlack, 1st Btn: 1854 – Sebastopol

Brevet-Major Gerald Littlehales Goodlake, 1st Btn: 1854 – Sebastopol

Private George Strong, 1st Btn: 1854 – Sebastopol

The Great War

Lance-Corporal George Henry Wyatt, 3rd Btn: 1914 – France

Lance-Corporal Frederick William Dobson, 2nd Btn: 1914 – France

Lance-Sergeant Oliver Brooks, 3rd Btn: 1915 – France

Temp. Lieutenant-Colonel John Vaughan Campbell, 3rd Btn: 1916 – France

Private Thomas Whitham, 1st Btn: 1917 – Belgium

Act. Captain Cyril Hubert Frisby, 1st Btn: 1918 – France

(P) Lance-Corporal Thomas Norman Jackson, 1st Btn: 1918 – France

2nd World War

Company Sergeant-Major Peter Harold Wright, 3rd Btn: 1943 – Italy

(P) Temp. Captain Ian Oswald Liddell, 5th Btn: 1945 – Germany

See also: 96

39. SCOTS GUARDS
(Formerly: SCOTS FUSILIER GUARDS)

Crimea

Brevet-Major Robert James Lindsay, 1st Btn: 1854 – The Alma

Lieutenant John Simpson Knox, 1st Btn: 1854 – The Alma
(Also: 1855 - Sebastopol, with The Rifle Brigade)

Sergeant James McKechnie, 1st Btn: 1854 – The Alma

Private William Reynolds, 1st Btn: 1854 – The Alma

Sergeant James Craig, 1st Btn: 1855 – Sebastopol
(later Ensign and Adjutant, Military Train)

The Great War

(P) Private James MacKenzie, 2nd Btn: 1914 – France

2nd Lieutenant George Arthur Boyd Rochfort, 1st Btn: Special Reserve: 1915 – France

Lance-Sergeant Frederick McNess, 1st Btn: 1916 – France

Sergeant John McAulay, 1st Btn: 1917 – France

Corporal Henry Blanshard Wood, 2nd Btn: 1918 – France

2nd World War

(P) Temp. Captain, The Lord Charles Anthony Lyell, 1st Btn: 1943 – Tunisia

40. IRISH GUARDS

The Great War

Lance-Corporal Michael O'Leary, 1st Btn: 1915 – France

Lance-Sergeant John Moyney, 2nd Btn: 1917 – Belgium

Private Thomas Woodcock, 2nd Btn: 1917 – Belgium

(P) Act. Lieutenant-Colonel John Neville Marshall, Special Reserve: 1918 – France
(Attached: 16th Btn. The Lancashire Fusiliers)

2nd World War

Lance-Corporal John Patrick Kenneally: 2nd Btn: 1943 – Tunisia

(P) Private Edward Colquhoun Charlton, 2nd Btn: 1945 – Germany

41. WELSH GUARDS

The Great War

Sergeant Robert James Bye, 1st Btn: 1917 – Belgium

2nd World War

(P) Lieutenant, The Hon. Christopher Furness, 1st Btn: 1940 – France

42. THE ROYAL SCOTS (THE ROYAL REGIMENT) (1st FOOT)

Crimea

Private Joseph Prosser, 2nd Btn: 1855 – Sebastopol

The Great War

Private Henry Howey Robson, 2nd Btn: 1914 – France

Private Robert Dunsire, 13th Btn: 1915 – France

Temp. Captain Henry Reynolds, 12th Btn: 1917 – Belgium

(P) Private Hugh McIver, 2nd Btn: 1918 – France

(P) Lieutenant David Stuart McGregor, 6th Btn TF: 1918 – Belgium
(Attached: 29th Machine-Gun Company)

Lance-Corporal Roland Edward Elcock, 11th Btn: 1918 – France

43. THE QUEEN'S ROYAL REGIMENT (WEST SURREY) (2nd FOOT)

West Africa

Lieutenant Wallace Duffield Wright, 1st Btn: 1903 – Nigeria
(Serving with The Northern Nigeria Regiment)

The Great War

Captain Bernard Cyril Freyberg: 1916 – France
(Commanding Hood Battalion, Royal Naval Division)

(P) Act. Captain Clement Robertson, Special Reserve: 1917 – Belgium
(With The Tank Corps)

(P) Lance-Corporal William Sayer, 8th Btn: 1918 – France

Temp. Lieutenant-Colonel Christopher Bushell, Special Reserve: 1918 – France
(Commanding 7th (Service) Btn)

2nd World War

(P) Lieutenant Alec George Horwood, 1/6th Btn: 1944 – Burma
(Attached: 1st Btn. The Northamptonshire Regiment)

44. THE EAST SURREY REGIMENT (31st/70th FOOT)

South Africa (Boer)

Private Albert Edward Curtis, 2nd Btn: 1900 – Paardeberg

The Great War

Lieutenant George Rowland Patrick Roupell, 1st Btn: 1915 – Belgium

2nd Lieutenant Benjamin Handley Greary, 4th Btn: 1915 – Belgium
(Attached: 1st Btn.)

Private Edward Dwyer, 1st Btn: 1915 – Belgium

Temp. 2nd Lieutenant Arthur James Terence Fleming-Sandes, 2nd Btn: 1915 – France

Sergeant Henry Cator, 7th Btn: 1917 – France

Corporal Edward Foster, 13th Btn: 1917 – France

(P) Corporal John McNamara, 9th Btn: 1918 – France

2nd World War

Act. Captain Eric Charles Twelves Wilson: 1940 – Somaliland
(Attached: Somali Mounted Infantry)

45. THE BUFFS (ROYAL EAST KENT) REGIMENT (3rd FOOT)

Crimea

Brevet Lieutenant-Colonel Frederick Francis Maude: 1855 – Sebastopol

Private John Connors: 1855 – Sebastopol

North West Frontier, India

Corporal James Smith, 1897 – Tirah

The Great War

Lance-Corporal William Reginald Cotter, 6th Btn: 1916 – France

See also: 88

46. THE ROYAL WEST KENT REGIMENT (QUEEN'S OWN) (50th/97th FOOT)

Crimea

Sergeant John Coleman, 97th Foot: 1855 – Sebastopol

Captain Charles Henry Lumley, 97th Foot: 1855 – Sebastopol

The Great War

(P) Sergeant Thomas James Harris, 6th Btn: 1918 – France

(P) Lieutenant Cecil Harold Sewell, 1918 – France
(Attached: 3rd (Light) Btn, The Tank Corps)

Temp. Lieutenant Donald John Dean, 8th Btn: 1918 – France

2nd World War

(P) Lance-Corporal John Pennington Harman, 4th Btn: 1944 – India

47. THE ROYAL SUSSEX REGIMENT (35th/107th FOOT)

New Zealand

Lieutenant-Colonel John Carstairs McNeill, 107th Foot: 1864 – Te Awamutu

The Great War

(P) Sergeant Henry Wells, 2nd Btn: 1915 – France

Temp. Lieutenant Eric Archibald McNair, 9th (S) Btn: 1916 – Belgium

(P) Company Sergeant-Major Nelson Victor Carter, 12th Btn: 1916 – France

2nd World War

(P) Captain Lionel Ernest Queripel: 1944 – Holland
(Attached: 10th Btn, The Parachute Regiment)

See also: 78

48. THE MIDDLESEX REGIMENT (DUKE OF CAMBRIDGE'S OWN) (57th/77th FOOT)

Crimea

Sergeant John Park, 77th Foot: 1854-55 – Alma, Inkerman, Sebastopol

Sergeant George Gardiner, 57th Foot: 1855 – Sebastopol

Private Alexander Wright, 77th Foot: 1855 – Sebastopol

Private Charles McCorrie, 57th Foot: 1855 – Sebastopol

New Zealand

Ensign John Thornton Down, 57th Foot: 1863 – Pontoko

Drummer Dudley Stagpoole, 57th Foot: 1863 – Pontoko

The Great War

(P) Temp. 2nd Lieutenant Rupert Price Hallowes, 4th Btn: 1915 – Belgium

Private Frederick Jeremiah Edwards, 12th Btn: 1916 – France

Private Robert Edward Ryder, 12th Btn: 1916 – France

(P) Act. Captain Allastair Malcolm Cluny McReady-Diarmid, 17th (S) Btn: 1917 – France
(Formerly: Arthur Malcolm McReady-Drew)

Act. Captain Alfred Maurice Toye, 2nd Btn: 1918 – France

49.   THE KING'S OWN (ROYAL LANCASTER) REGIMENT (4th FOOT)

Crimea

Private Thomas Grady: 1854 – Sebastopol

The Great War

Private Henry Christian, 2nd Btn: 1915 – France

(P) Private James Miller, 7th Btn: 1916 – France

Private Jack White, 6th Btn: 1917 – Mesopotamia
(Real name: Jacob Weiss)

Lance-Sergeant Thomas Fletcher Mayson, 4th Btn: 1917 – Belgium

Private Albert Halton, 1st Btn: 1917 – Belgium

(P) 2nd Lieutenant Joseph Henry Collin, 1/4th Btn: 1918 – France

Lance-Corporal James Hewitson, 1/4th Btn: 1918 – France

(P) Lance-Sergeant Thomas Neeley, 8th Btn: 1918 – France

50. THE BORDER REGIMENT
(34th/55th FOOT)

Crimea

Private Thomas Beach, 55th Foot: 1854 – Inkerman

Private William Coffey, 34th Foot: 1855 – Sebastopol

Brevet-Major Frederick Cockayne Elton, 55th Foot: 1855 – Sebastopol

Private John Joseph Sims, 34th Foot: 1855 – Sebastopol

Indian Mutiny

Private George Richardson, 34th Foot: 1859 – Trans Gogra

The Great War

Private Abraham Acton, 2nd Btn: 1914 – France

Private James Smith, 2nd Btn: 1914 – France
(Attached: 3rd Btn)

Sergeant Edward John Mott, 1st Btn: 1917 – France

Sergeant Charles Edward Spackman, 1st Btn: 1917 – France

Captain James Forbes-Robertson, 1st Btn: 1918 – France

51. THE ROYAL NORTHUMBERLAND FUSILIERS
(5th FOOT)

Indian Mutiny

Sergeant Robert Grant, 1857 – Lucknow

Private Peter McManus, 1857 – Lucknow

Private Patrick McHale, 1857 – Lucknow

The Great War

Lance-Corporal Thomas Bryan, 25th (S) Btn: 1917 – France

Private Ernest Sykes, 27th (S) Btn: 1917 – France

Temp. 2nd Lieutenant John Scott Youll, 1st Btn: 1918 – Ital
(Attached: 11th (S) Btn)

2nd Lieutenant James Johnson, 2nd Btn: 1918 – France
(Attached: 36th Btn)

Private Wilfred Wood, 10th Btn: 1918 – Italy

2nd World War

(P) Lieutenant James Joseph Bernard Jackman: 1941 – Tobruk

Temp. Major Robert Henry Cain: 1944 – Holland
(Attached: The South Staffordshire Regiment – 1st Airborne Division)

52. THE ROYAL WARWICKSHIRE REGIMENT (Later FUSILIERS) (6th FOOT)

The Great War

Private Arthur Vickers, 2nd Btn: 1915 – France

Temp. Lieutenant & Adjutant Robert Edwin Phillips, 13th Btn: 1917 – Mesopotamia
(Attached: 9th (S) Btn.)

Private Arthur Hutt, 1/7th Btn: 1917 – Belgium

(P) Lieutenant Julian Royds Gribble, 10th (S) Btn: 1918 – France

Lance-Corporal William Amey, 1/8th Btn TF: 1918 – France

53. THE ROYAL FUSILIERS (CITY OF LONDON REGIMENT) (7th FOOT)

Crimea

Private William Norman: 1854 – Sebastopol

Captain Henry Mitchell Jones: 1855 – Sebastopol

Private Matthew Hughes: 1855 – Sebastopol

Lieutenant William Hope: 1855 – Sebastopol

Assistant Surgeon Thomas Egerton Hale: 1855 – Sebastopol

Afghanistan

Private Thomas Elsdon Ashford: 1880 – Kandahar

South Africa (Boer)

Captain Charles Fitzclarence: 1899 – Mafeking
(Commanding a squadron of The Protectorate Regiment)

The Great War

(P) Lieutenant Maurice James Dease, 4th Btn: 1914 – Belgium

Private Sidney Frank Godley, 4th Btn: 1914 – Belgium

(P) Temp. Lieutenant Wilbur Taylor Dartnell, 25th (S) Btn, Frontiersmen: 1915 – Kenya

Lance-Sergeant Frederick William Palmer, 22nd Btn: 1917 – France

(P) Corporal George Jarratt, 8th Btn: 1917 – France

Sergeant John Molyneux, 2nd Btn: 1917 – Belgium

Lieutenant Robert Gee, 2nd Btn: 1917 – France

Captain Neville Elliott-Cooper, 8th Btn: 1917 – France

(P) Act. Captain Walter Napleton Stone, 3rd Btn: 1917 – France (Attached: 17th (S) Btn)

Lance-Corporal Charles Graham Robertson, 10th Btn: 1918 – Belgium

Corporal Arthur Percy Sullivan, 45th Btn: 1919 – North Russia

(P) Sergeant Samuel George Pearse, 45th Btn: 1919 – North Russia

See also: 12

54. THE LANCASHIRE FUSILIERS (20th FOOT)

The Great War

(P) Captain Cuthbert Bromley, 1st Btn: 1915 – Gallipoli

Captain Richard Raymond Willis, 1st Btn: 1915 – Gallipoli

Sergeant Alfred Joseph Richards, 1st Btn: 1915 – Gallipoli

(P) Sergeant Frank Edward Stubbs, 1st Btn: 1915 – Gallipoli

Corporal John Elisha Grimshaw, 1st Btn: 1915 – Gallipoli

(P) Private William Keneally, 1st Btn: 1915 – Gallipoli

(P) Private John Lynn, 2nd Btn: 1915 – Belgium

Private James Hutchinson, 5th Btn: 1916 – France

(P) Temp. Lieutenant-Colonel Bertram Best-Dunkley, 5th Btn: 1917 – Belgium

Sergeant Joseph Lister, 1st Btn: 1917 – Belgium

(P) 2nd Lieutenant Bernard Matthew Cassidy, 2nd Btn: 1918 – France

(P) Temp. 2nd Lieutenant John Schofield, 2/5th Btn: 1918 – France

Lance-Corporal Joel Halliwell, 11th Btn: 1918 – France

Corporal Edward Smith, 1/5th Btn: 1918 – France

(P) Private Harold John Colley, 10th Btn: 1918 – France

(P) Private Frank Lester, 10th Btn: 1918 – France

Sergeant James Clarke, 15th Btn: 1918 – France

2nd World War

Private Francis Arthur Jefferson, 2nd Btn: 1944 – Italy

See also: 40

55. THE KING'S (LIVERPOOL) REGIMENT (8th FOOT)

South Africa (Boer)

Sergeant Henry Hampton, 2nd Btn: 1900 – Vanwyksvlei

Corporal Henry James Knight, 1st Btn: 1900 – Vanwyksvlei
(with The 4th Mounted Infantry)

Private William Heaton, 1st Btn: 1900 – Geluk Farm

The Great War

Lance-Corporal Joseph Harcourt Tombs, 1st Btn: 1915 – France

(P) 2nd Lieutenant Edward Felix Baxter, 1/8th Btn: 1916 – France

Private Arthur Herbert Proctor, 1/5th Btn, TF: 1916 – France

(P) Sergeant David Jones, 12th Btn: 1916 – France

Captain Oswald Austin Reid, 1st Btn: 1917 – Mesopatamia
 (Attached: 6th Btn, The Loyal (North Lancashire) Regiment)

Private Jack Thomas Counter, 1st Btn: 1918 – France

See also: 81 131.

56. THE MANCHESTER REGIMENT (63rd/96th FOOT)

South Africa (Boer)

Private James Pitts, 1st Btn: 1900 – Ladysmith

Private Robert Scott, 1st Btn: 1900 – Ladysmith

The Great War

Lieutenant James Edgar Leach, 2nd Btn: 1914 – France

Sergeant John Hogan, 2nd Btn: 1914 – France

Act. Corporal Issy Smith, 1st Btn: 1915 – Belgium

Lieutenant William Thomas Forshaw, 1/9th Btn. TF: 1915 – Gallipoli

Private George Albert Stringer, 1st Btn: 1916 – Mesopotamia

Company Sergeant-Major William John George Evans, 18th Btn: 1916 – France

Sergeant Charles Henry Coverdale, 11th Btn: 1917 – Belgium

(P) Private Walter Mills, 1/10th Btn: 1917 – France

(P) Temp. Lieutenant-Colonel Wilfred Elstob, 16th Btn: 1918 – France

(P) 2nd Lieutenant James Kirk, 10th Btn: 1918 – France
(Attached: 2nd Btn)

Private Alfred Robert Wilkinson, 1/5th Btn TF: 1918 – France

Mesopotamia

(P) Captain George Stuart Henderson, 2nd Btn: 1920 – Hillah

See also: 132

57. THE ROYAL NORFOLK REGIMENT (9th FOOT)

The Great War

Act. Lieutenant-Colonel John Sherwood-Kelly: 1917 – France
(Commanding the 1st Btn. The Royal Inniskilling Fusiliers)

2nd World War

(P) Company Sergeant-Major George Gristock, 2nd Btn: 1940 – Belgium

(P) Temp. Captain John Neil Randle, 2nd Btn: 1944 – India

(P) Corporal Sidney Bates, 1st Btn: 1944 – France

Captain David Auldgo Jamieson, 7th Btn: 1944 – France

(P) Lieutenant George Arthur Knowland: 1945 – Burma
(Attached: No 1 Commando)

58. THE SUFFOLK REGIMENT (12th FOOT)

The Great War

Sergeant Arthur Frederick Saunders, 9th (S) Btn: 1915 – France

Corporal Sidney James Day, 11th Btn: 1917 – France

59. THE ROYAL LINCOLNSHIRE REGIMENT
(10th FOOT)

Indian Mutiny

Private John Kirk: 1857 – Benares

Lieutenant Henry Marshman Havelock: 1857 – Cawnpore

Private Denis Dempsey: 1857 – Lucknow

The Great War

Act. Corporal Charles Richard Sharpe, 2nd Btn: 1915 – France

Captain & Adjutant Percy Howard Hansen, 6th (S) Btn: 1915 – Gallipoli

Corporal Walter Simpson, 6th Btn: 1918 – France
(Arthur Walter Evans)

2nd World War

(P) Temp. Major Charles Ferguson Hoey, 1st Btn: 1944 – Burma

See also: 87 95 125

60. THE NORTHAMPTONSHIRE REGIMENT
(48th/58th FOOT)

Transvaal (Boer)

Lieutenant Alan Rickard Hill, 58th Foot: 1881 – Laing's Nek
(Later Hill-Walker)

Private James Osborne, 58th Foot: 1881 – Wesselstroom

The Great War

(P) Captain Anketell Moutray Read, 1st Btn: 1915 – France

Sergeant William Ewart Boulter, 6th Btn: 1916 – France

(P) Act. Captain Thomas Riversdale Colyer-Fergusson, 2nd Btn: 1917 – Belgium

(P) Lance-Corporal Allan Leonard Lewis, 6th Btn: 1918 – France

See also: 43 61 128

61. THE BEDFORDSHIRE AND HERTFORDSHIRE REGIMENT (16th FOOT)

The Great War

Captain Charles Calveley Foss, 2nd Btn: 1915 – France

(P) Private Edward Warner, 1st Btn: 1915 – Belgium

Temp. 2nd Lieutenant Thomas Edwin Adlam, 7th Btn: 1916 – France

Private Christopher Augustus Cox, 7th Btn: 1917 – France

(P) Act. Lieutenant-Colonel John Stanhope Collings-Wells, 4th Btn: 1918 – France

Private Samuel Needham, 1/5th Btn: 1918 – Palestine

Temp. 2nd Lieutenant Frederick William Hedges: 1918 – France
(Attached: 6th Btn, The Northamptonshire Regiment)

62. THE ESSEX REGIMENT (44th/56th FOOT)

Crimea

Sergeant William McWheeney, 44th Foot: 1854/55 - Sebastopol

China

Lieutenant Robert Mentrosor Rogers, 44th Foot: 1860 – Taku Forts
Private John McDougall, 44th Foot: 1860 – Taku Forts

South Africa (Boer)

Lieutenant Francis Newton Parsons, 1st Btn: 1900 – Paardeberg

The Great War

(P) 2nd Lieutenant Frank Bernard Wearne, 2rd Btn: 1917 – France
 (Attached: 11th Btn)

2nd World War

Lieutenant-Colonel Augustus Charles Newman: 1942 – France
(Attached: No 2 Commando)

63. THE ROYAL LEICESTERSHIRE REGIMENT (17th FOOT)

Crimea

Corporal Philip Smith: 1855 – Sebastopol

The Great War

Private William Buckingham, 2nd Btn: 1915 – France

(P) 2nd Lieutenant Philip Eric Bent, 9th Btn: 1917 – Belgium

Lieutenant John Cridlan Barrett, 5th Btn TF: 1918 – France

64. THE DEVONSHIRE REGIMENT (11th FOOT)

South Africa (Boer)

Lieutenant James Edward Ignatius Masterson, 1st Btn: 1900 – Ladysmith

The Great War

Private Theodore William Henry Veale, 8th Btn: 1916 – France

Lance-Corporal George Onions, 1st Btn: 1918 – France

65. THE DORSET REGIMENT (39th/54th FOOT)

North West Frontier, India

Private Samuel Vickery, 1st Btn: 1897 – Tirah

66. THE SOMERSET LIGHT INFANTRY (PRINCE ALBERT'S) (13th FOOT)

Indian Mutiny

Sergeant William Napier: 1858 – Azimghur

Private Patrick Carlin: 1858 – Azimghur

The Zulu War

Major William Knox Leet, 1st Btn: 1879 – Hlobane Mountain

The Great War

Private Thomas Henry Sage, 8th Btn: 1917 – Belgium

2nd World War

(P) Lieutenant George Albert Cairns: 1944 – Belgium
(Attached: The South Staffordshire Regiment)

67. THE DUKE OF CORNWALL'S LIGHT INFANTRY (32nd/46th FOOT)

Indian Mutiny

Corporal William Oxenham, 32nd Foot: 1857 – Lucknow

Private William Dowling, 32nd Foot: 1857 – Lucknow

Lieutenant Samuel Hill Lawrence, 32nd Foot: 1857 – Lucknow

Captain Henry George Browne, 32nd Foot: 1857 – Lucknow

Somaliland

Lieutenant Clement Leslie Smith, 2nd Btn: 1904 – Jidballi

The Great War

Bandsman Thomas Edward Rendle, 1st Btn: 1914 – Belgium

Korea

(P) Lieutenant Philip Kenneth Edward Curtis, 1st Btn: 1950 – The Imjin River
(Attached: 1st Btn, The Gloucestershire Regiment)

68. THE KING'S OWN YORKSHIRE LIGHT INFANTRY (51st/105th FOOT)

South Africa (Boer)

Private Charles Ward, 2nd Btn: 1900 – Lindley

The Great War

(P) Major Charles Allix Lovington Yate, 2nd Btn: 1914 – France

Lance-Corporal Frederick William Holmes, 2nd Btn: 1914 – France

(P) Private Horace Waller, 10th (S) Btn: 1917 – France

Sergeant John William Ormsby, 2nd Btn: 1917 – France

Private Wilfred Edwards, 7th Btn: 1917 – Belgium

(P) Act. Lieutenant-Colonel Oliver Cyril Spencer Watson: 1918 – France
(Reserve of Officers, Commanding 2/5th Btn.)

Sergeant Laurence Calvert, 5th Btn: 1918 – France

Act. Lieutenant-Colonel Harold Greenwood, 9th Btn: 1918 – France

69. THE KING'S SHROPSHIRE LIGHT INFANTRY (53rd/85th FOOT)

Indian Mutiny

Sergeant Denis Dynon, 53rd Foot: 1857 – Chota Bahar
(Serving with the 11th Bengal Native Infantry)

Lieutenant Alfred Kirk Ffrench, 53rd Foot: 1857 – Lucknow

Private Charles Irwin, 53rd Foot: 1857 – Lucknow

Private James Kenny, 53rd Foot: 1857 – Lucknow

Sergeant-Major Charles Pye, 53rd Foot: 1857 – Lucknow

The Great War

Private Harold Whitfield, 10th Btn: 1918 – Palestine

2nd World War

Sergeant George Harold Eardley, 4th Btn: 1944 – Holland

(P) Private James Stokes, 2nd Btn: 1945 – Rhineland

70. THE DURHAM LIGHT INFANTRY (68th/10th FOOT)

Crimea

Private John Byrne, 68th Foot: 1854-55 – Inkerman & Sebastopol

Captain Thomas de Courcy Hamilton, 68th Foot: 1855 – Sebastopol

New Zealand

Sergeant John Murray, 68th Foot: 1864 – Tauranga

The Great War

Private Thomas Kenny, 13th (S) Btn: 1915 – France

Lieutenant Roland Boys Bradford, 9th Btn: 1916 – France

Private Michael Heaviside, 15th Btn: 1917 – France

(P) Temp. 2nd Lieutenant Frederick Youens, 13th Btn: 1917 – Belgium

Act. Captain Arthur Moore Lascelles, 3rd Btn: 1917 – France

Private Thomas Young, 9th Btn: 1918 – France
(Real name Morrell)

2nd World War

2nd Lieutenant Richard Wallace Annand, 2nd Btn: 1940 – Belgium

(P) Private Adam Herbert Wakenshaw, 9th Btn: 1942 – Western Desert

71. THE WEST YORKSHIRE REGIMENT (THE PRINCE OF WALES'S OWN) (14th FOOT)

South Africa (Boer)

Captain Conwyn Mansel-Jones, 2nd Btn: 1900 – Natal

Sergeant William Bernard Traynor, 2nd Btn: 1901 – Bothwell Camp

The Great War

Corporal Samuel Meekosha, 6th Btn TF: 1915 – France
(Later known by the surname Ingram)

Corporal George Sanders, 7th Btn: 1916 – France

Private William Boynton Butler, 17th Btn: 1917 – France
(Attached: 106th Trench Mortar Battery)

Sergeant Albert Mountain, 15/17th Btn: 1918 – France

2nd World War

(P) Act. Sergeant Hanson Victor Turner, 1st Btn: 1944 – Burma

See Also: 73

72. THE EAST YORKSHIRE REGIMENT (DUKE OF YORK'S OWN) (15th FOOT)

The Great War

Private George William Chafer, 1st Btn: 1916 – France

(P) Private John Cunningham, 12th (S) Btn: 1916 – France

(P) Temp. 2nd Lieutenant John Harrison, 11th (S) Btn: 1917 – France

Sergeant Harold Jackson, 7th (S) Btn: 1918 – France

2nd World War

(P) Private Eric Anderson, 5th Btn: 1943 – Tunisia

73. THE GREEN HOWARDS (ALEXANDRA, PRINCESS OF WALES'S OWN REGIMENT OF YORKSHIRE) (19th FOOT)

Crimea

Private Samuel Evans, 1855 – Sebastopol

Private John Lyons: 1855 – Sebastopol

South Africa (Boer)

Sergeant Alfred Atkinson, 1st Btn: 1900 – Paardeberg

The Great War

Corporal William Anderson, 2nd Btn: 1915 – France

(P) Temp. Major Stewart Walter Loudoun-Shand, 10th Btn: 1916 – France

(P) Temp. 2nd Lieutenant Donald Simpson Bell, 9th Btn: 1916 – France

(P) Private William Short, 8th Btn: 1916 – France

Temp. Captain Archibald Cecil Thomas White, 6th Btn: 1916 – France

(P) 2nd Lieutenant David Philip Hirsch, 4th Btn: 1917 – France

Private Thomas Dresser, 7th Btn: 1917 – France

(P) Corporal William Clamp, 6th Btn: 1917 – Belgium

(P) Temp. 2nd Lieutenant Ernest Frederick Beale, 8th (S) Btn: 1918 – France

Sergeant William McNally, 8th (S) Btn: 1918 – Italy

2nd World War

(P) Temp. Lieutenant-Colonel Derek Anthony Seagrim, 7th Btn: 1943 – Tunisia

Company Sergeant-Major Stanley Elton Hollis, 6th Btn: 1944 – France

(P) Lieutenant William Basil Weston, 2nd Btn: 1945 – Burma
(Attached: 1st Btn. The West Yorkshire Regiment)

See Also: 91

74. THE ROYAL SCOTS FUSILIERS (21st FOOT)

South Africa (Boer)

Private George Ravenhill, 2nd Btn: 1899 – Colenso

The Great War

Private David Ross Lauder, 4th Btn: 1915 – Gallipoli

2nd Lieutenant John Manson Craig, 4th Btn: 1917 – Palestine

(P) 2nd Lieutenant Stanley Henry Parry Boughey, 1/4th Btn: 1917 – Palestine

Sergeant Thomas Caldwell, 13th Btn: 1918 – Belgium

2nd World War

(P) Private Dennis Donnini, 4/5th Btn: 1945 – Holland

75. THE HIGHLAND LIGHT INFANTRY (CITY OF GLASGOW REGIMENT) (71st/74th HIGHLANDERS)

Indian Mutiny

Private George Rodgers, 71st Highlanders: 1858 – Gwalior

Egypt

Lieutenant William Mordaunt Marsh Edwards, 2nd Btn: 1882 – Tel-el-Kabir

Sudan

Captain, The Hon. Alexander Gore Arkwright Hore-Ruthven, 3rd Btn: 1898 – Gedarif

South Africa (Boer)

Corporal John David Francis Shaul, 1st Btn: 1899 – Magersfontein

Private Charles Thomas Kennedy, 2nd Btn: 1900 – Dewetsdorp

The Great War

Private George Wilson, 2nd Btn: 1914 – France

Lieutenant Walter Lorrain Brodie, 2nd Btn: 1914 – Belgium

Lance-Corporal William Angus, 8th Btn TF: 1915 – France

(P) Sergeant James Young Turnbull, 17th Btn: 1916 – France

Private John Brown Hamilton, 9th Btn: 1917 – Belgium

(P) Temp. Major William Herbert Anderson, 12th (S) Btn: 1918 – France

Corporal David Ferguson Hunter, 1/5th Btn: 1918 – France

2nd World War

(P) Temp. Major Frank Gerald Blaker: 1944 – Burma
(Attached: 3rd Btn, 9th Gurkha Rifles)

See also: 102

76. THE CHESHIRE REGIMENT
(22nd FOOT)

The Great War

Private Thomas Alfred Jones, 1st Btn: 1916 – France

2nd Lietenant Hugh Colvin, 9th Btn: 1917 – Belgium

77. THE ROYAL WELCH FUSILIERS
(23rd FOOT)

Crimea

Sergeant Luke O'Connor, 1st Btn: 1854 – The Alma

Captain Edward William Derrington Bell, 1st Btn: 1854 – The Alma

Assistant Surgeon William Henry Thomas Sylvester, 1st Btn: 1855 – Sebastopol

Corporal Robert Shields, 1st Btn: 1855 – Sebastopol

Indian Mutiny

Lieutenant Thomas Bernard Hackett, 1st Btn: 1857 – Lucknow

Private George Monger, 1st Btn: 1857 – Lucknow

The Great War

(P) Lieutenant-Colonel Charles Hotham Montagu Doughty-Wylie: 1915 – Gallipoli (HQ Staff, Mediterranean Expeditionary Force)

Company Sergeant-Major Frederick Barter, Special Reserve: 1st Btn: 1915 – France

Corporal Joseph John Davies. 10th Btn: 1916 – France

Private Albert Hill, 10th Btn: 1916 – France

(P) Corporal James Llewellyn Davies, 13th Btn: 1917 – Belgium

Act. Corporal John Collins, 25th Btn: 1917 – Palestine

Lance-Corporal Edward Henry Weale, 14th Btn: 1918 – France

(P) Lance-Sergeant William Herbert Waring, 25th Btn. TF: 1918 – France

See also: 131

78. THE SOUTH WALES BORDERERS AND MONMOUTHSHIRE REGIMENT (24th FOOT)

The Bay of Bengal

Assistant Surgeon Campbell Mellis Douglas, 2nd Btn: 1867 – Little Andaman Island

Private David Bell, 2nd Btn. 1867 – Little Andaman Island

Private James Cooper, 2nd Btn: 1867 – Little Andaman Island

Private William Griffiths 2nd Btn: 1867 – Little Andaman Island

Private Thomas Murphy, 2nd Btn: 1867 – Little Andaman Island

Ashanti

Lieutenant, The Lord Edric Frederick Frederick Gifford, 2nd Btn: 1874 – Becquah

The Zulu War

(P) Lieutenant Teignmouth Melvill, 1st Btn: 1879 – Isandhlwana

(P) Lieutenant Neville Josiah Aylmer Coghill, 1st Btn: 1879 – Jsandhlwana

Lieutenant Gonville Bromhead, 2nd Btn: 1879 – Rorke's Drift

Corporal William Wilson Allen, 2nd Btn: 1879 – Rorke's Drift

Private Alfred Henry Hook, 2nd Btn: 1879 – Rorke's Drift

Private Robert Jones, 2nd Btn: 1879 – Rorke's Drift

Private William Jones, 2nd Btn: 1879 – Rorke's Drift

Private John Williams, 2nd Btn: 1879 – Rorke's Drift
(Real name: Fielding)

Lieutenant Edward Stevenson Browne, 1st Btn: 1879 – Hlobane Mountain

The Great War

Lieutenant Angus Buchanan, 4th Btn: 1916 Mesopotamia

Private James Henry Fynn, 4th Btn: 1916 – Mesopotamia

(P) Sergeant Albert White, 2nd Btn: 1917 – France

Sergeant Ivor Rees, 11th Btn: 1917 – Belgium

Company Sergeant-Major John Henry Williams, 10th Btn: 1918 – France

Temp. Lieutenant-Colonel Dudley Graham Johnson: 1918 – France
(Attached: 2nd Btn. The Royal Sussex Regiment)

2nd World War

Corporal Edward Thomas Chapman, 3rd Btn. The Monmouthshire Regiment: 1945 – Germany

See also: 85

79. THE WELCH REGIMENT
(41st/69th FOOT)

Crimea

Sergeant-Major Ambrose Madden, 41st Foot: 1854 – Little Inkerman

Captain Hugh Rowlands, 41st Foot: 1854 – Inkerman

The Great War

Lance-Corporal William Charles Fuller, 2nd Btn: 1914 – France

2nd Lieutenant Edgar Kinghorn Myles, 8th Btn: 1916 – Mesopotamia
(Attached: The Worcestershire Regiment)

Private Hubert William Lewis, 11th Btn. 1916 – Salonica

2nd World War

Lieutenant Tasker Watkins, 1/5th Btn: 1944 – France

80. THE KING'S OWN SCOTTISH BORDERERS (25th FOOT)

South Africa (Boer)

Lieutenant & Adjutant Gustavus Hamilton Blenkinsopp Coulson, 1st Btn: 1901 – Lambrechtfontein
(Attached: 7th Mounted Infantry)

The Great War

Piper Daniel Laidlaw, 7th Btn: 1915 – France

Sergeant William Henry Grimbaldeston, 1st Btn: 1917 – Belgium

Sergeant John Skinner, 1st Btn: 1917 – Belgium

(P) Act-Sergeant Louis McGuffie, 5th Btn. TF: 1918 – Belgium

See also: 95

81. THE CAMERONIANS (SCOTTISH RIFLES) (26th/90th FOOT)

Crimea

Private John Alexander, 90th Foot: 1855 – Sebastopol

Ensign Andrew Moynihan, 90th Foot: 1855 – Sebastopol
(Later served with the 8th Foot)

Indian Mutiny

Lieutenant William Rennie, 90th Foot: 1857 – Lucknow

Surgeon Anthony Dickson Home, 90th Foot: 1857 – Lucknow

Assistant-Surgeon William Bradshaw, 90th Foot: 1857 – Lucknow

Major John Christopher Guise, 90th Foot: 1857 – Lucknow

Sergeant Samuel Hill, 90th Foot: 1857 – Lucknow

Private Patrick Graham, 90th Foot: 1857 – Lucknow

The Zulu War

Lieutenant Henry Lysons, 90th Foot: 1879 – Hlobane Mountain

Private Edmund John Fowler, 90th Foot: 1879 – Hlobane Mountain

The Great War

Private Henry May, 1st Btn: 1914 – France

Act. Sergeant John Erskine, 5th Btn: 1916 – France

Private James Towers, 2nd Btn: 1918 – France

82. THE ROYAL INNISKILLING FUSILIERS (27th/108th FOOT)

The Great War

Captain Gerald Robert O'Sullivan, 1st Btn: 1915 – Gallipoli

Sergeant James Somers, 1st Btn: 1915 – Gallipoli

(P) Temp. Captain Eric Norman Frankland Bell, 9th Btn: 1916 – France (Attached: 109th Light Mortar Battery)

(P) Temp. 2nd Lieutenant James Samuel Emerson, 9th Btn: 1917 – France

Private James Duffy, 6th Btn: 1917 – Palestine

(P) Lance-Corporal Ernest Seaman, 2nd Btn: 1918 – Belgium

Private Norman Harvey, 1st Btn: 1918 – Belgium

See also: 57 131

83. THE ROYAL ULSTER RIFLES (Formerly THE ROYAL IRISH RIFLES) (83rd/86th FOOT)

Indian Mutiny

Lieutenant & Adjutant Hugh Stuart Cochrane, 86th Foot: 1858 – Jhansi

Captain Henry Edward Jerome, 86th Foot: 1858 – Jhansi

Private James Byrne, 86th Foot: 1858 – Jhansi

Private James Pearson, 86th Foot: 1858 – Jhansi

The Great War

(P) Private William Frederick McFadzean, 14th Btn: 1916 – France

Private Robert Quigg, 12th Btn: 1916 – France

(P) 2nd Lieutenant Edmund De Wind, 15th Btn: 1918 – France

84. THE ROYAL IRISH FUSILIERS (PRINCESS VICTORIA'S) (87th/89th FOOT)

The Great War

Private Robert Morrow, 1st Btn: 1915 – Belgium

(P) Temp. Lieutenant Geoffrey St George Shillington Cather, 9th Btn: 1916 – France

85. THE GLOUCESTERSHIRE REGIMENT (28th/61st FOOT)

Indian Mutiny

Surgeon Herbert Taylor Reade, 61st Foot: 1857 – Delhi

The Great War

(P) Temp. 2nd Lieutenant Hardy Falconer Parsons, 14th (S) Btn: 1917 – France

Temp. Captain Manley Angell James, 8th (S) Btn: 1918 – France

Major Daniel Burgess: 1918 – The Balkans
(Commanding 7th (S) Btn. The South Wales Borderers)

Private Francis George Miles, 5th Btn. TF: 1918 – France

Korea

Lieutenant-Colonel James Power Carne, 1st Btn: 1950 – The Imjin River

See also: 9 67.

86. THE WORCESTERSHIRE REGIMENT (29th/36th FOOT)

The Great War

2nd Lieutenant Herbert James, 4th Btn: 1915 – Gallipoli

Private Thomas George Turrall, 10th Btn: 1916 – France

Lieutenant William Leefe Robinson, 1916 – England
(Serving with 29 Squadron, The Royal Flying Corps)

Temp. Lieutenant Eugene Paul Bennett, 2nd Btn: 1916 – France

Private Frederick George Dancox, 4th Btn. 1918 – Belgium

Act. Lieutenant-Colonel Frank Crowther Roberts, 1st Btn: 1918 – France

2nd Lieutenant John James Crowe, 2nd Btn: 1918 – Belgium

Temp. Brigadier-General George William St George Grogan: 1918 – France
(Commanding the 23rd Infantry Brigade)
See also: 79

87. THE SHERWOOD FORESTERS (NOTTINGHAMSHIRE & DERBYSHIRE REGIMENT) (45th/95th FOOT)

Indian Mutiny

Private Bernard McQuirt, 95th Foot: 1858 – Rowa

North West Frontier, India

Lieutenant Henry Singleton Pennell, 2nd Btn: 1897 – Tirah

South Africa (Boer)

Corporal Henry Churchill Beet, 1st Mounted Infantry: 1900 – Wakkerstroom
Private William Bees, 1st Btn: 1901 – Moodwil

The Great War

Private Jacob Rivers, 1st Btn: 1915 – France

Corporal James Upton, 1st Btn: 1915 – France

2nd Lieutenant Charles Geoffrey Vickers, 7th Btn. TF: 1915 – France

(P) Temp. Captain Albert Ball: 7th Btn: 1916/17 – For Services with The Royal Flying Corps

Corporal Ernest Albert Egerton, 16th Btn: 1917 – Belgium

Act. Corporal Frederick Greaves, 9th Btn: 1917 – Belgium

Captain Charles Edward Hudson, 11th Btn: 1918 – Italy

(P) Act. Lieutenant-Colonel Bernard William Vann, 8th Btn: 1918 – France
(Attached: 6th Btn)

Sergeant William Henry Johnson, 5th Btn. TF: 1918 – France

2nd World War

(P) Temp. Captain John Henry Cound Brunt, 1944 – Italy
(Attached: 6th Btn. The Lincolnshire Regiment)
See also: 131.

88. THE EAST LANCASHIRE REGIMENT (30th/59th FOOT)

Crimea

Lieutenant Mark Walker, 30th Foot: 1854 – Inkerman
(Later served with the 3rd Buffs)

Afghanistan

Captain Euston Henry Sartorius, 59th Foot: 1879 – Shahjui

The Great War

Drummer Spencer John Bent, 1st Btn: 1914 – Belgium

Private William Young, 8th (S) Btn: 1915 – France

(P) 2nd Lieutenant Alfred Victor Smith, 5th Btn. TF: 1915 – Gallipoli

(P) 2nd Lieutenant Basil Arthur Horsfall, 3rd Btn: 1918 – France
(Attached: 11th Btn)

2nd World War

Captain Harold Marcus Ervine-Andrews, 1st Btn: 1940 – France

89. THE PRINCE OF WALES'S VOLUNTEERS (THE SOUTH LANCASHIRE REGIMENT) (40th/82nd FOOT)

New Zealand

Colour-Sergeant John Lucas, 40th Foot: 1861 – Huirangi Bush

The Great War

2nd Lieutenant Gabriel George Coury, 3rd Btn: 1916 – France
(Attached: 1/4th Btn)

Private John Readitt, 6th Btn: 1917 – Mesopotamia

Private William Ratcliffe, 2nd Btn: 1917 – Belgium

Corporal John Thomas Davies, 11th Btn: 1918 – France

90. THE LOYAL REGIMENT (NORTH LANCASHIRE) (47th/81st FOOT)

Crimea

Private John McDermond, 47th Foot: 1854 – Inkerman

The Great War

Private Henry Edward Kenny, 1st Btn: 1915 – France

(P) Lieutenant Richard Basil Brandram Jones, 8th Btn: 1915 – France

(P) Lieutenant Thomas Orde Lauder Wilkinson, 7th Btn: 1916 – France

2nd World War

(P) Lieutenant Wilwood Alexander Sandys-Clarke, 1st Btn: 1943 – Tunisia

See also: 55 125

91. THE DUKE OF WELLINGTON'S REGIMENT (WEST RIDING) (33rd/76th FOOT)

Abyssinia

Drummer Michael Magner, 33rd Foot: 1868 – Magdala

Private James Bergin, 33rd Foot: 1868 – Magdala

South Africa (Boer)

Sergeant James Firth, 1st Btn: 1900 – Arundel

The Great War

Lieutenant Henry Kelly, 10th Btn: 1916 – France

Private Arnold Loosemore, 8th Btn: 1917 – Belgium

Private Arthur Poulter, 1/4th Btn: 1918 – France

Private Henry Tandey, 5th Btn: 1918 – France
(Formerly served with The Green Howards)

2nd Lieutenant James Palmer Huffam, 5th Btn. TF: 1918 – France
(Attached: 2nd Btn)

2nd World War

Private Richard Henry Burton, 1st Btn: 1944 – Italy

92. THE ROYAL HAMPSHIRE REGIMENT (37th/67th FOOT)

China

Lieutenant Edmund Henry Lenon, 67th Foot: 1860 – Taku Forts

Lieutenant Nathaniel Burslem, 67th Foot: 1860 – Taku Forts

Ensign John Worthy Chaplin, 67th Foot: 1860 – Taku Forts

Private Thomas Lane, 67th Foot: 1860 – Taku Forts

The Great War

2nd Lieutenant George Raymond Dallas Moor, 3rd Btn: 1915 – Dardanelles

2nd Lieutenant Denis George Wyldbore Hewitt, 14th Btn: 1917 – Belgium

2nd Lieutenant Montague Shedworth Seymour Moore, 15th Btn: 1917 – Belgium

2nd World War

Captain Herbert Wallace Le Patourel, 2nd Btn: 1942 – Tunisia

Temp. Captain Richard Wakeford, 4th Btn: 1944 – Italy

See also: 182 206

93. THE SOUTH STAFFORDSHIRE REGIMENT (38th/80th FOOT)

The Zulu War

Private Samuel Wassall, 80th Foot: 1879 – Isandhlwana

Colour-Sergeant Anthony Clarke Booth, 80th Foot: 1879 – Ntombi River

The Great War

(P) Captain John Franks Vallentin, 1st Btn: 1914 – Belgium

(P) Captain Arthur Forbes Gordon Kilby, 2nd Btn: 1915 – France

(P) Private Thomas Barratt, 7th Btn: 1917 – Belgium

2nd World War

(P) Lance-Sergeant John Daniel Baskeyfield: 1944 – Holland
(Attached: 1st Airborne Division)

See also: 4 51 66

94. THE NORTH STAFFORDSHIRE REGIMENT (THE PRINCE OF WALES'S) (64th/98th FOOT)

Indian Mutiny

Drummer Thomas Flinn, 64th Foot: 1857 – Cawnpore

The Great War

(P) Major Edward Elers Delavel Henderson: 1917 – Mesopotamia
(Attached: 9th Btn. The Royal Warwickshire Regiment)

Sergeant John Carmichael, 9th Btn: 1917 – Belgium

Private John Thomas, 5th Btn: 1917 – France

Private William Harold Coltman, 1/6th Btn. TF: 1917 – France

95. THE BLACK WATCH (ROYAL HIGHLAND REGIMENT) (42nd/73rd HIGHLANDERS)

Indian Mutiny

Lieutenant Francis Edward Henry Farquharson, 42nd Highlanders: 1858 – Lucknow

Quartermaster-Sergeant John Simpson, 42nd Highlanders: 1858 – Ruhya

Lance-Corporal Alexander Thompson, 42nd Highlanders: 1858 – Ruhya

Private James Davis, 42nd Highlanders: 1858 – Ruhya

(P) Private Edward Spence, 42nd Highlanders: 1858 – Ruhya

Colour-Sergeant William Gardner, 42nd Highlanders: 1858 – Ruhya

Private Walter Cook, 42nd Highlanders: 1858 – Central India

Private Duncan Millar, 42nd Highlanders: 1858 – Central India

Ashanti

Lance-Sergeant Samuel McGaw, 42nd Highlanders: 1874 – Amoaful

Sudan

Private Thomas Edwards, 1st Btn: 1884 – Tamai

The Great War

Corporal John Ripley, 1st Btn: 1915 – France

Lance-Corporal David Finlay, 2nd Btn: 1915 – France

Private Charles Melvin, 2nd Btn: 1917 – Mesopotamia

Major Lewis Pugh Evans: 1917 – Belgium
(Commanding 1st Btn. The Lincolnshire Regiment)

Korea

Private William Speakman, 1st Btn: 1951 – Yonchon
(Attached: 1st Btn. The King's Own Scottish Borderers)

See Also: 216

96. THE ROYAL BERKSHIRE REGIMENT (PRINCESS CHARLOTTE OF WALES'S) (49th/66th FOOT)

Crimea

Lieutenant John Augustus Conolly, 49th Foot: 1854 – Sebastopol
(Later served with The Coldstream Guards)

Corporal James Owens, 49th Foot: 1854 – Sebastopol

Sergeant George Walters, 49th Foot: 1854 – Inkerman

South Africa (Boer)

Private William House, 2nd Btn: 1900 – Mosiliatse Nek

The Great War

(P) 2nd Lieutenant Alexander Buller Turner, 3rd Btn: 1915 – France
(Attached: 1st Btn)

Lance-Corporal James Welch, 1st Btn: 1917 – France

See also: 131

97. THE WILTSHIRE REGIMENT (DUKE OF EDINBURGH'S) (62nd/99th FOOT)

The Great War

Act. Captain Reginald Frederick Johnson Hayward, 1st Btn: 1918 – France

2nd World War

(P) Sergeant Maurice Albert Windham Rogers, 2nd Btn: 1944 – Italy

61

98.   THE YORK AND LANCASTER REGIMENT (65th/84th FOOT)

Indian Mutiny

Lance-Corporal Abraham Boulger, 84th Foot: 1857 – Lucknow

Sergeant-Major George Lambert, 84th Foot: 1857 – Lucknow

Private Joel Holmes, 84th Foot: 1857 – Lucknow

Captain Augustus Henry Archibald Anson, 84th Foot: 1857 – Bolundshahur & Lucknow

Lance-Corporal John Sinnott, 84th Foot: 1857 – Lucknow

Private William Patrick Mylott, 84th Foot: 1857 – Lucknow

New Zealand

Colour-Sergeant Edward MacKenna, 65th Foot: 1863 – Cameron Town

Lance-Corporal John Ryan, 65th Foot: 1863 – Cameron Town

The Great War

Private Samuel Harvey, 1st Btn: 1915 – France

Private John Caffrey, 2nd Btn: 1915 – France

(P) Sergeant Frederick Charles Riggs, 6th Btn: 1918 – France

Corporal John Brunton Daykins, 4th Btn. TF: 1918 – France

2nd World War

(P) Corporal John William Harper, 4th Btn: 1944 – Belgium

99.   SEAFORTH HIGHLANDERS (ROSS-SHIRE BUFFS, THE DUKE OF ALBANY'S) (72nd/78th HIGHLANDERS)

Indian Mutiny

Lieutenant Andrew Cathcart Bogle, 78th Highlanders: 1857 – Lucknow

Lieutenant Joseph Petrus Hendrick Crowe, 78th Highlanders: 1857 – Lucknow

Lieutenant Herbert Taylor MacPherson, 78th Highlanders: 1857 – Lucknow

Surgeon Joseph Jee, 78th Highlanders: 1857 – Lucknow

Assistant-Surgeon Valentine Mumbee McMaster, 78th Highlanders: 1857 – Lucknow

Private Henry Ward, 78th Highlanders: 1857 – Lucknow

Colour-Sergeant Stewart MacPherson, 78th Highlanders: 1857 – Lucknow

Private John Hollowell, 78th Highlanders: 1857 – Lucknow

Lieutenant Aylmer Spicer Cameron, 72nd Highlanders: 1858 – Kotah

Afghanistan

Lance-Corporal George Sellar, 72nd Highlanders: 1879 – Kabul

Ashanti

Sergeant John MacKenzie, 2nd Btn: 1900 – Dompoassi
(Employed with The West African Frontier Force)

The Great War

Corporal Sidney William Ware, 1st Btn: 1916 – Mesopotamia

Drummer Walter Potter Ritchie, 2nd Btn: 1916 – France

Lance-Sergeant Thomas Steele, 1st Btn: 1917 – Mesopotamia

Lieutenant Donald MacKintosh, 3rd Btn: 1917 – France

Sergeant Alexander Edwards, 6th Btn: 1917 – Belgium

Lance-Corporal Robert McBeath, 5th Btn: 1917 – France

(P) Sergeant John Meikle, 4th Btn: 1918 – France

See also: 216

100. QUEEN'S OWN CAMERON HIGHLANDERS (79th HIGHLANDERS)

South Africa (Boer)

Sergeant Donald Dickson Farmer, 1st Btn: 1900 – Nooitgedacht

The Great War

Private Ross Tollerton, 1st Btn: 1914 – France

(P) Lieutenant-Colonel Angus Falconer Douglas-Hamilton, Reserve of Officers: Commanding the 6th Btn: 1915 – France

Corporal James Dalgleish Pollock, 5th Btn: 1915 – France

See also: 216

101. GORDON HIGHLANDERS
(75th/92nd HIGHLANDERS)

Indian Mutiny

Colour-Sergeant Cornelius Coghlan, 75th Highlanders: 1857 – Delhi

Ensign Richard Wadeson, 75th Highlanders: 1857 – Delhi

Private Patrick Green, 75th Highlanders: 1857 – Delhi

Afghanistan

Major George Stuart White, 92nd Highlanders: 1879/80 – Charasia/Kandahar

Lieutenant William Henry Dick-Cunyngham, 92nd Highlanders: 1879 – Kabul

North West Frontier, India

Piper George Findlater, 1st Btn: 1897 – Tirah

Private Edward Lawson, 1st Btn: 1897 – Tirah

South Africa (Boer)

Captain Matthew Fontaine Maury Meiklejohn, 2nd Btn: 1899 – Elandslaagte

Sergeant-Major William Robertson, 2nd Btn: 1899 – Elandslaagte

Captain Ernest Beachcroft Beckwith Towse, 1st Btn: 1899/1900 – Magersfontein/Mount Thapa

Corporal John Frederick Mackay, 1st Btn: 1900 – Johannesberg

Captain William Eagleson Gordon, 1st Btn: 1900 – Krugersdorp

Captain David Reginald Younger, 1st Btn: 1900 – Krugersdorp

The Great War

Drummer William Kenny, 2nd Btn: 1914 – Belgium

(P) Captain James Anson Otho Brooke, 2nd Btn: 1914 – Belgium

Private George Imlach McIntosh, 1/6th Btn: 1917 – Belgium

Lieutenant Allan Ebenezer Ker, 3rd Btn: 1918 – France
(Attached: The Machine-Gun Corps)

See also: 122 (Notes)

102. ARGYLL AND SUTHERLAND HIGHLANDERS (PRINCESS LOUISE'S) (91st/93rd HIGHLANDERS)

Indian Mutiny

Captain William George Drummond Stewart, 93rd Highlanders: 1857 – Lucknow

Colour-Sergeant James Munro, 93rd Highlanders: 1857 – Lucknow

Sergeant John Paton, 93rd Highlanders: 1857 – Lucknow

Lance-Corporal John Dunley, 93rd Highlanders: 1857 – Lucknow

Private Peter Grant, 93rd Highlanders: 1857 – Lucknow

Private David Mackay, 93rd Highlanders: 1857 – Lucknow

Lieutenant William McBean, 93rd Highlanders: 1858 – Lucknow

The Great War

Captain John Aiden Liddell, 3rd Btn: 1915 – Belgium

Lieutenant John Reginald Noble Graham, 9th Btn: 1917 – Mesopotamia
(Attached: 136th Machine Gun Corps)

(P) 2nd Lieutenant Arthur Henderson, 4th Btn: 1917 – France

(P) 2nd Lieutenant John Crawford Buchan, 7th Btn: 1918 – France
(Attached: 8th Btn. TF)

Temp. 2nd Lieutenant David Lowe McIntyre: 1918 – France
(Attached: 1/6th Btn. Highland Light Infantry)

Lieutenant William Davidson Bissett, 6th Btn. TF: 1918 – France

2nd World War

Temp. Lieutenant-Colonel Lorne MacLaine Campbell, 7th Btn: 1943 – Tunisia

Act. Major John Thompson McKellar Anderson, 8th Btn: 1943 – Tunisia

Korea

(P) Major Kenneth Muir, 1st Btn: 1950 – Songju

103. THE PARACHUTE REGIMENT (AND AIRBORNE FORCES)

2nd World War

(P) Lieutenant John Hollington Grayburn, 2nd Btn: 1944 – Holland

The Falkland Islands

(P) Lieutenant-Colonel Herbert 'H' Jones, 2nd Btn: 1982 – Goose Green

(P) Sergeant Ian John McKay, 3rd Btn: 1982 – Mount Longdon

See Also: 4 47 51 93 216

104. 2nd KING EDWARD VII'S OWN GURKHA RIFLES (THE SIRMOOR RIFLES)

2nd World War

Subadar Lalbahadur Thapa, 1st Btn: 1943 – Tunisia

Rifleman Bhanbhagta Gurung, 3rd Btn: 1945 – Burma

See also: 132

105. 3rd QUEEN ALEXANDRA'S OWN GURKHA RIFLES

The Great War

Rifleman Kulbir Thapa, 2nd Btn: 1915 – France

Rifleman Karanbahadur Rana, 2nd Btn: 1918 – Egypt

106. 5th ROYAL GURKHA RIFLES

2nd World War

Havildar Gaje Ghale, 2nd Btn: 1943 – Burma

Naik Agansingh Rai, 2nd Btn: 1944 – Burma

(P) Act. Subadar Netrabahadur Thapa, 2nd Btn: 1944 – Burma

(P) Rifleman Thaman Gurung, 1st Btn: 1944 – Burma

See also: 132

107. 6th QUEEN ELIZABETH'S OWN GURKHA RIFLES

2nd World War

Rifleman Tulbahadur Pun, 3rd Btn: 1944 – Burma

See also: 29

108. 7th DUKE OF EDINBURGH'S OWN GURKHA RIFLES

2nd World War

Rifleman Ganju Lama, 1st Btn: 1944 – Burma

109. 8th GURKHA RIFLES

2nd World War

Rifleman Lachhiman Gurung, 4th Btn: 1945 – Burma
See also: 132

110. 9th GURKHA RIFLES

The Great War

Major George Campbell Wheeler, 2nd Btn: 1917 – Mesopotamia

2nd World War

(P) Rifleman Sherbahadur Thapa, 1st Btn: 1944 – Italy
See also: 75

111. 10th PRINCESS MARY'S OWN GURKHA RIFLES

Malaya

Lance-Corporal Rambahadur Limbu, 2nd Btn: 1965 – Sarawak

112. THE OXFORDSHIRE AND BUCKINGHAMSHIRE LIGHT INFANTRY (43rd/52nd FOOT)

Indian Mutiny

Bugler Robert Hawthorne, 52nd Foot: 1857 – Delhi
Lance-Corporal Henry Smith, 52nd Foot: 1857 – Delhi
Private Henry Addison, 43rd Foot: 1858 – Central India

New Zealand

Captain Frederick Augustus Smith, 43rd Foot: 1864 – Tauranga

The Great War

Company Sergeant-Major Edward Brooks, 4th Btn: 1917 – France

Lance-Corporal Alfred Wilcox, 2/4th Btn: 1918 – France

113. THE KING'S ROYAL RIFLE CORPS (60th RIFLES)

Indian Mutiny

Private Samuel Turner, 1st Btn: 1857 – Delhi

Colour-Sergeant Stephen Garvin, 1st Btn: 1857 – Delhi

Private James Thompson, 1st Btn: 1857 – Delhi

Private John Divane, 1st Btn: 1857 – Delhi

Bugler William Sutton, 1st Btn: 1857 – Delhi

Colour-Sergeant George Waller, 1st Btn: 1857 – Delhi

Lieutenant Alfred Spencer Heathcote, 1st Btn: 1857 – Delhi

Private Valentine Bambrick, 1st Btn: 1858 – Bareilly

The Zulu War

Captain And Brevet Lieutenant-Colonel Redvers Henry Buller: 1879 – Hlobane Mountain

Egypt

Private Frederick Corbett, 3rd Btn: 1882 – Kafr Dowar
(Alias David Embleton)

Sudan

Lieutenant Percival Scrope Marling, 3rd Btn: 1884 – Tamai

South Africa (Boer)

Lieutenant, The Hon. Frederick Hugh Sherston Roberts: 1899 – Colenso

Lieutenant Llewellyn Alberic Emilius Price-Davies: 1901 – Transvaal

The Great War

Lieutenant John Henry Stephen Dimmer, 2nd Btn: 1914 – Belgium

Captain John Fitzhardinge Paul Butler: 1914 – Cameroons
(Attached: The Gold Coast Regiment, West African Frontier Force)

Private William Mariner, 2nd Btn: 1915 – France
(Real name Wignall)

(P) Private George Stanley Peachment, 2nd Btn: 1915 – France

(P) Sergeant Albert Gill, 1st Btn: 1916 – France

Sergeant Edward Cooper, 12th Btn: 1917 – France

Private Albert Edward Shepherd, 12th (S) Btn: 1917 – France

2nd World War

(P) Private John Beeley, 1st Btn: 1941 – Tobruk

See also: 131

114. THE RIFLE BRIGADE (PRINCE CONSORT'S OWN)

Crimea

Lieutenant, The Hon. Henry Hugh Clifford, 1st Btn: 1854 – Inkerman

Private Francis Wheatley, 1st Btn: 1854 – Sebastopol

Brevet-Major Claud Thomas Bourchier, 1st Btn: 1854 – Sebastopol

Captain William James Montgomery Cunninghame, 1st Btn: 1854 – Sebastopol

Private Joseph Bradshaw, 2nd Btn: 1855 – Sebastopol

Private Robert Humpston, 2nd Btn: 1855 – Sebastopol

Private Roderick McGregor, 2nd Btn: 1855 - Sebastopol

Indian Mutiny

Captain Henry Wilmot, 2nd Btn: 1858 – Lucknow

Corporal William Nash, 2nd Btn: 1858 – Lucknow

Private David Hawkes, 2nd Btn: 1858 – Lucknow

Private Same Shaw, 3rd Btn: 1858 – Lucknow

Canada

Private Timothy O'Hea, 1st Btn: 1866 – Danville Station

South Africa (Boer)

Captain Walter Norris Congreve, 1899 – Colenso
(HQ Staff, The Natal Field Force)

Private Edward Durrant, 2nd Btn: 1900 – Bergendal

Somaliland

Captain John Edmond Gough, 1903 – Daratoleh

The Great War

Company Sergeant-Major Harold Daniels, 2nd Btn: 1915 – France

Act. Corporal Cecil Reginald Noble, 2nd Btn: 1915 – France

(P) 2nd Lieutenant Sidney Clayton Woodroffe, 8th Btn: 1915 – Belgium

(P) Corporal Alfred George Drake, 8th Btn: 1915 – France

(P) Brevet-Major William La Touch Congreve, 1916 – France
(Brigade-Major, 76th Infantry Brigade)

(P) 2nd Lieutenant George Edward Cates, 2nd Btn: 1917 – Belgium

Sergeant William Francis Burman, 16th Btn: 1917 – Belgium

Lance-Sergeant Joseph Edward Woodall, 1st Btn: 1918 – France

Sergeant William Gregg, 13th Btn: 1918 – France

Private William Beesley, 13th Btn: 1918 – France

2nd World War

Temp. Lieutenant-Colonel Victor Buller Turner, 1942 – Western Desert
See also: 39 131

115. SPECIAL FORCES

2nd World War

(P) Temp. Major Anders Frederik Emil Victor Schau Lassen: 1945 – Italy
(General List, Attached: Special Boat Service/No 1 Special Air Service)
See also: 57 62

116. THE ROYAL IRISH REGIMENT
   (18th FOOT)

Crimea

Captain Thomas Esmonde: 1855 – Sebastopol

New Zealand

Captain Hugh Shaw: 1865 – Nukumaru

South Africa (Boer)

(P) Private John Barry, 1st Btn: 1901 – Transvaal

The Great War

Private Frederick George Room, 2nd Btn: 1917 – Belgium

117. THE CONNAUGHT RANGERS (88th/94th FOOT)

South Africa (Basuto)

Major Hans Garrett Moore, 88th Foot: 1877 – Komgha
Private Thomas Flawn, 94th Foot: 1879 – Sekukuni's Town
Private Francis Fitzpatrick, 94th Foot: 1877 – Sekukuni's Town

Transvaal (Boer)

Lance-Corporal James Murray, 2nd Btn: 1881 – Elandsfontein

The Great War

Private Thomas Hughes, 6th Btn: 1916 – France

118. THE PRINCE OF WALES'S LEINSTER REGIMENT (ROYAL CANADIANS) (100th/109th FOOT)

Indian Mutiny

Private Frederick Whirlpool, 109th Foot: 1858 – Jhansi
(The 109th were formerly the 3rd Bombay European Regiment)

The Great War

Lieutenant John Vincent Holland, 3rd Btn: 1916 – France
(P) Corporal John Cunningham, 2nd Btn: 1917 – France
Sergeant John O'Niell, 2nd Btn: 1918 – Belgium
Private Martin Moffatt, 2nd Btn: 1918 – Belgium

119. THE ROYAL MUNSTER FUSILIERS (101st/104th FOOT)

Indian Mutiny

Lieutenant Thomas Cadell, 104th Foot: 1857 – Delhi
(The 104th were formerly the 2nd Bengal European Fusiliers)

Private John McGovern, 101st Foot: 1857 – Delhi
(The 101st were formerly the 1st Bengal European Fusiliers)

Sergeant James McGuire, 101st Foot: 1857 – Delhi

Drummer Miles Ryan, 101st Foot: 1857 – Delhi

Lieutenant Francis David Millet Brown, 101st Foot: 1857 – Narnaul

Lieutenant Thomas Adair Butler, 101st Foot: 1858 – Lucknow

The Great War

Corporal William Cosgrove, 1st Btn: 1915 – Gallipoli

Lieutenant Arthur Hugh Batten-Pooll, 3rd Btn: 1916 – France

Company Sergeant-Major Martin Doyle, 1st Btn: 1918 – France

See also: 4

120. THE ROYAL DUBLIN FUSILIERS (102nd/103rd FOOT)

Indian Mutiny

Sergeant Patrick Mahoney, 102nd Foot: 1857 – Lucknow
(The 102nd were formerly the 1st Madras European Fusiliers)

Private Thomas Duffy, 102nd Foot: 1857 – Lucknow

Private John Ryan, 102nd Foot: 1857 – Lucknow

Private John Smith, 102nd Foot: 1857 – Lucknow

The Great War

Sergeant Robert Downie, 2nd Btn: 1916 – France

Sergeant James Ockenden, 1st Btn: 1917 – Belgium

Sergeant Horace Augustus Curtis, 2nd Btn: 1918 – France

121. THE LONDON REGIMENT
   (TERRITORIAL FORCE)

The Great War

2nd Lieutenant Geoffrey Harold Woolley, 9th Btn: 1915 – Belgium

Lance-Sergeant Douglas Walter Belcher, 1/5th Btn: 1915 – Belgium

Lance-Corporal Leonard James Keyworth, 24th Btn: 1915 – France

Sergeant Alfred Joseph Knight, 2/8th Btn: 1917 – Belgium

Lieutenant-Colonel Arthur Drummond Borton, 2/22nd Btn: 1917 – Palestine

Private John Alexander Christie, 1/4th Btn: 1917 – Palestine

Private Jack Harvey, 1/22nd Btn: 1918 – France

See also: 27, 122 (Notes)

122. THE LONDON SCOTTISH REGIMENT
   (TERRITORIAL FORCE)

The Great War

Corporal Charles William Train, 2/14th Btn: 1917 – Palestine

Private Robert Edward Cruickshank, 2/14th Btn: 1918 – Palestine

2nd World War

(P) Private George Allan Mitchell, 1st Btn: 1944 – Italy

See Also: 122 (Notes)

123. THE HERTFORDSHIRE REGIMENT
   (TERRITORIAL FORCE)

The Great War

Corporal Alfred Alexander Burt, 1st Btn: 1915 – France

(P) 2nd Lieutenant Frank Edward Young, 1st Btn: 1918 – France

124. THE WEST INDIA REGIMENT

West Africa

Private Samuel Hodge, 1st Btn: 1866 – Gambia

West Africa

Lance-Corporal William James Gordon, 4th Btn: 1892 – Toniataba

125. THE ROYAL ARMY CHAPLAINS' DEPARTMENT

The Great War

The Reverend Edward Noel Mellish, Temp. CF: 1916 – France
(Attached: The Royal Fusiliers)

The Reverend William Robert Fountaine Addison, Temp. CF: 1916 – Mesopotamia
(Attached: 6th Btn. The Loyal Regiment)

The Reverend Theodore Bayley Hardy, Temp. CF: 1918 – France
(Attached: The Lincolnshire Regiment)

See also: 186

126. MILITARY TRAIN

Indian Mutiny

Private Samuel Morley, 2nd Btn: 1858 – Azimghur

Private Michael Murphy, 2nd Btn: 1858 – Azimghur

See also: 34 39

127. COMMISSARIAT AND TRANSPORT CORPS

The Zulu War

Act. Assistant Commissariat Officer James Langley Dalton: 1879 – Rorke's Drift

128. THE ROYAL ARMY SERVICE CORPS

The Great War

Private Richard George Masters: 1918 – France
(Attached: 141st Field Ambulance)

Temp. 2nd Lieutenant Alfred Cecil Herring: 1918 – France
(Attached: 6th (S) Btn. The Northamptonshire Regiment)

129. THE ARMY HOSPITAL CORPS

Transvaal (Boer)

Prov. Lance-Corporal Joseph John Farmer: 1881 – Majuba Hill

130. THE ARMY MEDICAL SERVICE

The Zulu War

Surgeon James Henry Reynolds: 1879 – Rorke's Drift

Upper Burma

Surgeon Ferdinand Simeon Le Quesne: 1889 – Tartan

Burma

Surgeon-Major Owen Edward Pennefather Lloyd: 1893 – Simla

131. THE ROYAL ARMY MEDICAL CORPS

South Africa (Boer)

Lieutenant Henry Edward Manning Douglas: 1899 – Magersfontein

Major William Babtie: 1899 – Colenso

Lieutenant Edgar Thomas Inkson: 1900 – Arundel
(Attached: The Royal Inniskilling Fusiliers)

Lieutenant William Henry Snyder Nickerson: 1900 – Wakkerstroom
(Attached: The Mounted Infantry)

The Great War

(P) Captain Henry Sherwood Ranken: 1914 – France
(Attached: 1st Btn. The King's Royal Rifle Corps)

Lieutenant Arthur Martin-Leake: 1914 – Belgium
(Attached: 5th Field Ambulance)
(This was a bar to his VC gained with the South African Constabulary during the Boer
War – See 200)

Temp. Lieutenant George Allan Maling: 1915 – France
(Attached: 12th Btn. The Rifle Brigade)

(P) Captain John Leslie Green: 1916 – France
(Attached: 1/5th Btn. The Sherwood Foresters)

(P) Captain Noel Godfrey Chavasse: 1916 – France
(Attached: 1/10th Btn. The King's (Liverpool) Regiment)
(Captain Chavasse later gained a bar to his VC: 1917 – Belgium)

Captain William Barnsley Allen: 1916 – France
(Attached: 246th Royal Field Artillery)

(P) Temp. Captain Harold Ackroyd: 1917 – Belgiu
(Attached: 6th Btn. The Royal Berkshire Regiment)

Captain John Fox-Russell: 1917 – Palestine
(Attached: 1/6th Btn. The Royal Welch Fusiliers)

2nd World War

(P) Lance-Corporal Henry Eric Harden: 1945 – Holland
(Attached: The Royal Marine Commando)

For other British Medical Services and forces of the Crown see: 11 34 53 77 78 81
85 99 182 191 192 200 218 223

132. THE INDIAN STAFF CORPS, THE BENGAL STAFF CORPS, and THE BOMBAY STAFF CORPS

India

Major Donald Macintyre (Bengal): 1872 – Lalgnoora
(Serving with the 2nd Gurkha Regiment)

Malaya

Captain George Nicholas Channer (Bengal): 1875 – Perak
(Serving with the 1st Gurkha Light Infantry)

India (Beluchistan)

Captain Andrew Scott (Bengal): 1877 – Quetta
(Serving in the 4th Sikh Regiment)

Afghanistan

Captain John Cook (Bengal): 1878 – Peiwar Kotal
(Serving with the 5th Gurkha Rifles)

(P) Lieutenant Walter Richard Pollock Hamilton (Bengal): 1879 – Futtehabad
(Serving with The Queen's Own Corps of Guides)

Captain O'Moore Creagh (Bombay): 1879 – Kabul River
(Serving with the Marwara Btn)

Captain Arthur George Hammond (Bengal): 1879 – Kabul
(Serving with The Queen's Own Corps of Guides)

Captain William John Vousden (Bengal): 1879 – Kabul
(Serving with The 5th Punjab European Cavalry)

Lieutenant William St Lucien Chase (Bombay): 1880 – Kandahar
(Serving with the 28th Native Infantry)

North West Frontier, India

Captain Richard Kirby Ridgeway (Bengal): 1879 – Konoma
(Formerly with the 96th Foot – Serving with the 44th Gurkha Rifles)

Upper Burma

Lieutenant Charles James William Grant (Indian): 1891 – Manipur
(Serving with the 1/8th Gurkha Rifles)

North West Frontier, India

Lieutenant Guy Hudleston Boisragon (Indian): 1891 – Hunza

Lieutenant John Manners Smith (Indian): 1891 – Hunza
(Both serving with the 5th Gurkha Rifles)

North West Frontier, India

Lieutenant Edward William Costello (Indian): 1897 – Malakand
(Serving with the 22nd Punjab Infantry)

North West Frontier, India

Major Robert Bellew Adams (Indian): 1897 – Tirah
(Serving with The Queen's Own Corps of Guides)

(P) Lieutenant Hector Lachlan Stewart McLean (Indian): 1897 – Tirah
(Serving with The Queen's Own Corps of Guides)

South Africa (Boer)

Lieutenant Francis Aylmer Maxwell (Indian): 1900 – Korn Spruit
(Attached: to Roberts's Light Horse)

Ashanti

Captain Charles John Mellis (Indian): 1900 – Obassa
(Employed with The West African Frontier Force)

Somaliland

Captain Alexander Stanhope Cobbe (Indian): 1902 – Erego
(Employed with the 1st Btn. The King's African Rifles)

Captain George Murray Rolland (Indian): 1903 – Daratoleh
(Serving with the 1st Bombay Grenadiers/The Berbera Bohottle Flying Column)

Captain William George Walker (Indian): 1903 – Daratoleh
(Serving with the 4th Gurkha Rifles. Attached: Bikanir Camel Corps.)

Lieutenant Herbert Augustine Carter (Indian): 1903 – Jidballa
(6th Indian Mounted Infantry, attached: The King's African Rifles)

Tibet

Lieutenant John Duncan Grant (Indian): 1904 – Gyantse Jong
(Serving with the 8th Gurkha Rifles)

133. 1st PUNJAB CAVALRY

Indian Mutiny

Lieutenant John Watson: 1857 – Lucknow

134. 2nd PUNJAB CAVALRY

Indian Mutiny

Captain Dighton MacNaughten Probyn: 1857 – Lucknow

135. 2nd BOMBAY LIGHT CAVALRY

Indian Mutiny

Captain James Blair: 1857 – Central India

136. 3rd BOMBAY LIGHT CAVALRY

Persia

Lieutenant And Adjutant Arthur Thomas Moore: 1857 – Bozdar
Lieutenant John Grant Malcolmson: 1857 – Bozdar

137. 5th BENGAL EUROPEAN CAVALRY

Indian Mutiny

Major Charles John Stanley Gough: 1857 – Rhotuck

138. 6th BENGAL EUROPEAN CAVALRY

Ashanti

Major Reginald William Sartorius: 1874 – Abagoo

139. 7th HARIANA LANCERS

The Great War

(P) Major George Godfrey Massy Wheeler: 1915 – Mesopotamia

140. 14th MURRAY'S JAT HORSE (BENGAL LANCERS)

The Great War

(P) Ressaidar Badlu Singh: 1917 – France
(Attached: 29th Lancers, Deccan Horse)

141. 28th LIGHT CAVALRY

The Great War

Lance-Defadar Gobind Singh: 1917 – France
(Attached: 2nd Lancers)

142. 34th PRINCE ALBERT VICTOR'S OWN POONA HORSE

The Great War

(P) Lieutenant Frank Alexander De Pass: 1914 – France

143. 1st PUNJABI REGIMENT

2nd World War

(P) Jemadar Ram Serup Singh, 2nd Btn: 1944 – Burma

144. 2nd BENGAL NATIVE INFANTRY

Indian Mutiny

Colonel James Travers: 1857 – Central India

145. 4th BENGAL EUROPEAN REGIMENT

India

Lieutenant George Vincent Fosbury: 1863 – Umbeyla
(Attached: 1st Punjabi Infantry)

146. 4th PUNJABI INFANTRY

India

Lieutenant And Adjutant Henry William Pitcher: 1863 – Umbeyla

147. 4th BENGAL NATIVE INFANTRY

Indian Mutiny

Lieutenant Frederick Robertson Aikman: 1858 – Lucknow

148. 5th MAHRATTA LIGHT INFANTRY

2nd World War

(P) Naik Yeshwant Ghadge: 1944 – Italy
Sepoy Namdeo Jadhao: 1945 – Italy

149. 6th RAJPUTANA RIFLES

2nd World War

(P) Subadar Richhpal Ram: 1941 – Abyssinia
(P) Company-Havildar-Major Chhelu Ram: 1943 – Tunisia

150. 8th PUNJABI REGIMENT

2nd World War

Havildar Parkash Singh, 5th Btn: 1943 – Mayu Peninsula

Sepoy Kamal Ram. 3rd Btn: 1944 – Italy

151. 9th BHOPAL INFANTRY

The Great War

Sepoy Chatta Singh: 1916 – Mesopotamia

152. 9th JAT INFANTRY

2nd World War

(P) Jemadar Abdul Hafiz: 1944 – Burma

153. 10th BALUCHI REGIMENT

2nd World War

Sepoy Bhandari Ram: 1944 – Burma
(P) Act. Naik Fazal Din: 1945 – Burma

154. 11th BENGAL NATIVE INFANTRY

Indian Mutiny

(P) Ensign Everard Aloysius Lisle Phillipps: 1857 – Delhi
Lieutenant John Charles Campbell Daunt: 1857 – Chota Bahar
See Also: 69

155. 11th SIKH REGIMENT

2nd World War

Act. Naik Nand Singh, 1st Btn: 1944 – Burma

156. 12th FRONTIER FORCE RIFLES

North West Frontier, India

(P) Captain Godfrey Meynell, 5th Btn: 1935 – Mahmund
(Serving with The Queen's Own Corps Of Guides)

2nd World War

Lieutenant-Colonel Arthur Edward Cumming, 2nd Btn: 1942 – Malaya

157. 13th FRONTIER FORCE RIFLES

2nd World War

(P) Jemadar Prakash Singh, 14th Btn: 1945 – Burma
Sepoy Ali Haidar, 14th Btn: 1945 – Italy

158. 13th BENGAL NATIVE INFANTRY

Indian Mutiny

Lieutenant William George Cubitt: 1857 – Lucknow
Lieutenant Robert Hope Moncrieff Aitken: 1857 – Lucknow

159. 15th LUDHIANA SIKHS

Indian Mutiny

Sergeant-Major Peter Gill: 1857 – Benares

The Great War

Lieutenant John George Smyth: 1915 – France

160. 15th PUNJABI REGIMENT

2nd World War

Naik Gian Singh: 1945 – Burma
(P) Lieutenant Karamjeet Singh Judge: 1945 – Burma

161. 16th PUNJABI REGIMENT

2nd World War

(P) Lance-Naik Sher Shah: 1945 – Burma

162. 19th MADRAS NATIVE INFANTRY

Indian Mutiny

Captain Herbert Macworth Clogstoun: 1859 – Central India

163. 20th BOMBAY NATIVE INFANTRY

Persia

Captain John Augustus Wood: 1856 – Bushire

164. 24th BOMBAY NATIVE INFANTRY

Indian Mutiny

Lieutenant William Alexander Kerr: 1857 – Kolapore

165. 25th BOMBAY LIGHT INFANTRY

Indian Mutiny

Lieutenant William Francis Frederick Waller: 1858 – Gwalior

166. 26th BENGAL NATIVE INFANTRY

Indian Mutiny

Lieutenant Hanson Chambers Jarrett: 1858 – Central India

167. 28th PUNJABI REGIMENT

North West Frontier, India

Sepoy Ishar Singh: 1921 – Wazıristan

168. 37th BENGAL NATIVE INFANTRY

Indian Mutiny

Sergeant-Major Matthew Rosamond: 1857 – Benares

169. 39th GARHWALI RIFLES

The Great War

Naik Darwan Singh Negi: 1914 – France
(P) Rifleman Gobar Singh Negi: 1915 – France

North West Frontier, India

(P) Lieutenant William David Kenny: 1920 – Waziristan

170. 41st DOGRAS

The Great War

Lance-Naik Lala: 1916 – Mesopotamia

171. 46th BENGAL NATIVE INFANTRY

Indian Mutiny

Lieutenant-Colonel Samuel James Browne: 1858 – Central India

172. 51st SIKHS (FRONTIER FORCE)

Afghanistan

Captain Eustace Jotham: 1915 – Tochi Valley

173. 55th COKE'S RIFLES (FRONTIER FORCE)

The Great War

Jemadar Mir Dast: 1915 – Belgium
(Attached: 57th Wilde's Rifles)

174. 56th PUNJABI RIFLES (FRONTIER FORCE)

Indian Mutiny

Captain William Martin Cafe: 1858 – Central India

175 59th SCIND RIFLES

The Great War

(P) Lieutenant William Arthur McRae Bruce: 1914 – France

176. 60th BENGAL NATIVE INFANTRY

Indian Mutiny

Brevet-Captain Robert Haydon Shebbeare: 1857 – Delhi

177. 66th BENGAL NATIVE INFANTRY

Indian Mutiny

Lieutenant John Adam Tytler: 1858 – Oudh

178. 72nd BENGAL NATIVE INFANTRY

Indian Mutiny

Lieutenant Henry Hammon Lyster: 1858 – Central India

179. 89th PUNJABIS

The Great War

Naik Shahamad Khan: 1914 – Belgium

180. 129th DUKE OF CONNAUGHT'S OWN BALUCHIS

The Great War

Sepoy Khudadad Khan: 1914 – Belgium

181. THE BENGAL ARMY (UNATTACHED)

Indian Mutiny

Ensign Patrick Roddy: 1858 – Kuthirga

182. THE INDIAN MEDICAL SERVICE

China

Hospital Apprentice Andrew Fitzgibbon: 1860 – Taku Forts
(Attached: 2nd Btn. The Royal Hampshire Regiment)

Upper Burma

Surgeon John Crimmin: 1889 – Lwekow
(The Bombay Medical Service)

North West Frontier, India

Surgeon-Captain Henry Frederick Whitchurch: 1895 – Chitral

The Great War

Captain John Alexander Sinton: 1916 – Mesopotamia

North West Frontier, India

(P) Temp. Captain Henry John Andrews: 1919 – Waziristan

183. THE INDIAN ARMY ORDNANCE DEPARTMENT (BENGAL ESTABLISHMENT)

Indian Mutiny

Deputy Assistant Commissary John Buckley: 1857 – Delhi
Conductor James Miller: 1857 – Futtehpore

184. BENGAL POLICE BATTALION

Indian Mutiny

Lieutenant Charles George Baker: 1858 – Central India

185. BENGAL VETERAN'S ESTABLISHMENT

Indian Mutiny

Captain George Forrest: 1857 – Delhi
Captain William Raynor: 1857 – Delhi

186. THE BENGAL ECCLESIASTICAL ESTABLISHMENT (CIVILIAN)

Afghanistan

The Reverend James Williams Adams: 1879 – Killa Kazi

187. THE BENGAL CIVIL SERVICE

Indian Mutiny

Mr William Fraser McDonell: 1857 – Arrah

Mr Ross Lewis Mangles: 1857 – Arrah

Mr Thomas Henry Kavanagh: 1857 – Lucknow

188. THE SOUTH AFRICAN AIR FORCE

2nd World War

(P) Captain Edwin Swales: 1945 – Germany
(Serving with 582 Squadron, RAF.)

189. THE FRONTIER LIGHT HORSE

The Zulu War

Captain Henry Cecil Dudgeon D'Arcy: 1879 – Ulundi

Sergeant Edmund O'Toole: 1879 – Ulundi

190. THE NATAL NATIVE CONTINGENT

The Zulu War

Corporal Ferdnand Christian Schiess: 1879 – Rorke's Drift

191. THE CAPE MOUNTED RIFLES

South Africa (Basuto)

Sergeant Robert George Scott: 1879 – Moirosi's Mountain

Trooper Peter Brown: 1879 – Moirosi's Mountain

Surgeon-Major Edmund Barron Hartley: 1879 – Moirosi's Mountain

192. THE CAPE MOUNTED YEOMANRY (1st REGIMENT)

South Africa (Basuto)

Surgeon John Frederick McCrea: 1881 – Tweefontein

193. NOURSE'S TRANSVAAL HORSE

Transvaal (Boer)

Trooper John Danaher: 1881 – Elandsfontein

194. THE MASHONALAND MOUNTED POLICE

Rhodesia

Captain Randolph Cosby Nesbitt: 1896 – Mashonaland

195. THE BULAWAYO FIELD FORCE

Rhodesia

Trooper Herbert Stephen Henderson: 1896 – Bulawayo
(P) Trooper Frank William Baxter: 1896 – Bulawayo

196. THE PROTECTORATE REGIMENT (NORTH WEST CAPE COLONY)

South Africa (Boer)

Sergeant Horace Robert Martineau: 1899 – Mafeking
Trooper Horace Edward Ramsden: 1899 – Mafeking
See Also: 53

197. RIMINGTON'S GUIDES

South Africa (Boer)

Corporal John James Clements: 1901 – Cape Colony

198. THE CAPE POLICE

South Africa (Boer)

Sergeant-Major Alexander Young: 1901 – Ruiter's Kraal

199. THE SOUTH AFRICAN CONSTABULARY

South Africa (Boer)

Sergeant James Rogers: 1901 – Orange Free State
Surgeon-Captain Arthur Marin-Leake: 1902 – Vlakfontein
See Also: 131

200. THE IMPERIAL LIGHT HORSE (NATAL)

South Africa (Boer)

Captain Charles Herbert Mullins: 1899 – Elandslaagt
Captain Robert Johnston: 1899 – Elandslaagt
Trooper Herman Albrecht: 1900 – Ladysmith
Surgeon-Captain Thomas Joseph Crean: 1901 – Tygerskloof

201. SCOUT'S CORPS (2nd SOUTH AFRICAN MOUNTED BRIGADE)

The Great War

Captain William Anderson Bloomfield: 1916 – East Africa

202. THE SOUTH AFRICAN LIGHT INFANTRY

The Great War

Private William Frederick Faulds: 1st Btn: 1916 – France
Lance-Corporal William Henry Hewitt, 2nd Btn: 1917 – Belgium

203. THE BRITISH SOUTH AFRICAN POLICE

The Great War

Sergeant Frederick Charles Booth: 1917 – East Africa
(Attached: The Rhodesia Native Regiment)

204. THE KING'S AFRICAN RIFLES

2nd World War

(P) Sergeant Nigel Grey Leakey, 1/6th Btn: 1941 – Abyssinia
See Also: 132

205. THE ROYAL NATAL CARBINEERS

2nd World War

Sergeant Quentin George Murray Smythe: 1942 – Western Desert

206. THE KAFFIARIAN RIFLES

2nd World War

Lieutenant Gerard Ross Norton: 1944 – Italy
(Attached: 1/4th Btn. The Royal Hampshire Regiment)

207. THE ROYAL CANADIAN NAVAL VOLUNTEER RESERVE

2nd World War

(P) Lieutenant Robert Hampton Gray: 1945 – Japan
(Serving with 1841 Squadron, The Fleet Air Arm)

208. THE ROYAL CANADIAN AIR FORCE

2nd World War

(P) Pilot-Officer Andrew Charles Mynarski: 1944 – France
(Serving with 419 Squadron, RCAF.)

(P) Flight-Lieutenant David Ernest Hornell: 1944 – Atlantic Ocean
(Serving with 162 Squadron, RCAF. Coastal Command)

209. ROYAL CANADIAN DRAGOONS

South Africa (Boer)

Lieutenant Hampden Zane Churchill Cockburn: 1900 – Komati River
Lieutenant Richard Ernest William Turner: 1900 – Komati River

Sergeant Edward James Gibson Holland: 1900 – Komati River

210. LORD STRATHCONA'S CORPS (CANADIAN CAVALRY)

South Africa (Boer)

Sergeant Arthur Herbert Lindsay Richardson: 1900 – Transvaal

The Great War

Lieutenant Frederick Maurice Watson Harvey: 1917 – France

(P) Lieutenant Gordon Muriel Flowerdew: 1918 – France

211. THE FORT GARRY HORSE (CANADIAN CAVALRY)

The Great War

Lieutenant Harcus Strachan: 1917 – France

212. THE CANADIAN MACHINE GUN CORPS

The Great War

(P) Lieutenant Hugh McKenzie: 1917 – Belgium

213. THE CANADIAN ARMOURED CORPS

2nd World War

Major David Vivian Currie: 1944 – France
(29th Canadian Armoured Reconnaissance Regiment-South Alberta)

214. CANADIAN ENGINEERS

The Great War

Captain Coulson Norman Mitchell: 1st Tunnelling Company, 4th Btn: 1918 – France

215. CANADIAN MOUNTED RIFLES (INFANTRY)

The Great War

Captain William Avery Bishop: 1917 – France
(Serving with 60th Squadron, Royal Flying Corps)

Private Thomas William Holmes, 4th CMR (2nd Central Ontario). 1917 – Belgium

Act. Major George Randolph Pearkes, 5th CMR (Quebec): 1917 – Belgium

Lieutenant Charles Smith Rutherford 5th CMR (Quebec): 1918 – France

Temp. Captain John MacGregor, 2nd CMR (1st Central Ontario). 1918 – France

216. CANADIAN INFANTRY CORPS

The Great War

(P) Lance-Corporal Frederick Fisher, (13th Quebec): 1915 – Belgium
(Allied to the Black Watch: The Royal Highlanders of Canada)

(P) Company Sergeant-Major Frederick William Hall, (8th Manitoba): 1915 – Belgium

Captain Edward Donald Bellew, (7th British Columbia): 1915 – Belgium

(P) Lieutenant Frederick William Campbell, (1st Western Ontario): 1915 – Belgium

Act. Corporal Leo Clarke, (2nd Eastern Ontario): 1916 – France

Private John Chipman Kerr, (49th Alberta): 1916 – France

(P) Piper James Cleland Richardson, (16th Manitoba): 1916 – France
(Attached: The Canadian Scottish)

(P) Lance-Sergeant Ellis Welwood Sifton, (18th Western Ontario): 1917 – France

(P) Private William Johnstone Milne, (16th Manitoba): 1917 – France
(The Canadian Scottish)

Captain Thain Wendell MacDowell, (38th Eastern Ontario): 1917 – France
(Allied to The Cameron Highlanders of Canada)

(P) Private John George Pattison, (50th Alberta): 1917 – France

(P) Lieutenant Robert Grierson Combe, (27th Manitoba): 1917 – France

(P) Sergeant Frederick Hobson, (20th Central Ontario): 1917 – France

Private Michael James O'Rourke, (7th British Columbia): 1917 – France

(P) Private Henry Brown, (10th Quebec): 1917 – France

(P) Captain Okill Massey Learmonth, (2nd Eastern Ontario): 1917 – France

Company Sergeant-Major Robert Hill Hanna, (29th British Columbia): 1917 – France

Act. Corporal Filip Konowal, (47th British Colombia): 1917 – France

Lieutenant Robert Shankland, (43rd Manitoba): 1917 – Belgium
(Allied to The Cameron Highlanders of Canada)

Act. Captain Christopher Patrick John O'Kelly, (52nd Manitoba): 1917 – Belgium

Private Cecil John Kinross, (49th Alberta): 1917 – Belgium

Sergeant George Henry Mullin (Eastern Onterio): 1917 – Belgium
(Princess Patricia's Canadian Light Infantry)

Corporal Colin Fraser Barron, (3rd Central Ontario): 1917 – Belgium

(P) Private James Peter Robertson, (27th Manitoba): 1917 – Belgium

Lieutenant George Burdon McKean, (14th Quebec): 1918 – France

(P) Corporal Joseph Kaeble, (22nd Quebec): 1918 – France
(The Canadien Francais)

Corporal Herman James Good, (13th Quebec): 1918 – France
(Allied to The Black Watch: The Royal Highlanders of Canada)

(P) Private John Bernard Croak, (13th Quebec): 1918 – France
(Allied to The Black Watch: The Royal Highlanders of Canada)

(P) Corporal Henry Garnet Bedford Miner, (58th Central Ontario): 1918 – France

(P) Lieutenant John Brilliant, (22nd Quebec): 1918 – France
(The Canadien Francais)

(P) Lieutenant James Edward Tait, (78th Manitoba): 1918 – France
(The Winnipeg Grenadiers)

(P) Sergeant Raphael Louis Zengel, (5th Saskatchewan): 1918 – France

Corporal Frederick George Coppins, (8th Manitoba): 1918 – France

Act. Corporal Alexander Picton Brereton, (8th Manitoba): 1918 – France

Private Thomas Dinesen, (42nd Quebec): 1918 – France
(Allied to The Black Watch: The Royal Highlanders of Canada)

(P) Sergeant Robert East Spall, (Eastern Ontario): 1918 – France
(Princess Patricia's Canadian Light·Infantry)

Lieutenant-Colonel William Hew Clark-Kennedy (24th Quebec): 1918 – France
(Allied to The Black Watch: The Royal Highlanders of Canada)

Private Claud Joseph Patrick Nunney, (38th Eastern Ontario): 1919 – France
(Allied to The Cameron Highlanders of Canada)

Lieutenant-Colonel Cyrus Wesley Peck, (16th Manitoba): 1918 – France
(The Canadian Scottish)

Lance-Corporal William Henry Metcalf, (16th Manitoba): 1918 – France
(The Canadian Scottish)

(P) Sergeant Arthur George Knight, (10th Alberta): 1918 – France

Private John Francis Young, (87th Quebec): 1918 – France
(The Canadian Grenadier Guards)

Private Walter Leigh Rayfield, (7th British Columbia): 1918 – France

Lieutenant George Fraser Kerr, (3rd Central Ontario): 1918 – France

Lieutenant Graham Thomas Lyall, (2nd Central Ontario): 1918 – France

Lieutenant Milton Fowler Gregg, (40th Nova Scotia): 1918 – France
(Allied to The Black Watch: The Royal Highlanders of Canada)

(P) Lieutenant Samuel Lewis Honey, (78th Manitoba): 1918 – France
(The Winnipeg Grenadiers)

Sergeant William Merrifield (4th Central Ontario): 1918 – France

(P) Lieutenant Wallace Lloyd Algie, (1st Central Ontario): 1918 – France

(P) Sergeant Hugh Cairns, (46th Saskatchewan): 1918 – France

2nd World War

(P) Warrant Officer, Class II John Robert Osborne: (1st Btn. The Winnipeg Grenadiers) 1941 – Hong Kong

Lieutenant-Colonel Charles Cecil Ingersoll Merritt, (South Saskatchewan): 1942 – France

Act. Major Paul Triquet, (The Royal 22e Regiment): 1943 – Italy

Major John Keefer Mahoney, (The Westminster Regiment-Motor): 1944 – Italy

Private Ernest Alvia Smith, (Seaforth Highlanders of Canada): 1944 – Italy

(P) Sergeant Aubrey Cosens, (The Queen's Own Rifles of Canada) 1945 – Holland

Act. Major Frederick Tilston, (The Essex-Scottish Regiment): 1945 – Germany

Corporal Frederick George Topham, (1st Canadian Parachute Regiment): 1945 – Germany
(Attached to the British Airborne Forces)

217. THE CANADIAN CHAPLAINS' SERVICE

2nd World War

Hon. Captain John Wier Foote: 1942 – France
(Attached: The Royal Hamilton Light Infantry)

218. THE CANADIAN ARMY MEDICAL SERVICE

The Great War

Captain Francis Alexander Caron Scrimger: 1915 – Belgium
(Attached: Medical Officer, 14th Quebec Regiment)

Captain Bellenden Seymour Hutcheson: 1918 – France
(Attached: 75th Central Ontario Regiment)

219. THE ROYAL NEWFOUNDLAND REGIMENT

The Great War

Private Thomas Ricketts, 1st Btn: 1918 – France

220. THE ROYAL AUSTRALIAN AIR FORCE (AUSTRALIAN FLYING CORPS)

The Great War

Lieutenant Frank Hubert McNamara, 1st Squadron, AFC: 1917 – Egypt

2nd World War

(P) Pilot Officer Rawdon Hume Middleton: 1942 – Italy
(Serving with 149 Squadron, RAF)
(P) Flight-Lieutenant William Ellis Newton, 22 Squadron, RAAF: 1943 – New Guinea

221. 5th AUSTRALIAN FIELD ARTILLERY

2nd World War

Lieutenant Arthur Roden Cutler: 1941 – Syria

222. TASMANIAN IMPERIAL BUSHMEN

South Africa (Boer)

Lieutenant Guy George Egerton Wylly: 1900 – Transvaal
Private John Hutton Bisdee: 1900 – Transvaal

223. THE NEW SOUTH WALES MEDICAL STAFF CORPS

South Africa (Boer)

Captain Neville Richard Howse: 1900 – Orange Free State

224. WEST AUSTRALIAN MOUNTED INFANTRY

South Africa (Boer)

Lieutenant Frank William Bell: 1901 – Transvaal

225. 5th VICTORIAN MOUNTED RIFLES

South Africa (Boer)

Lieutenant Leslie Cecil Maygar: 1901 – Geelhoutboom

226. 10th AUSTRALIAN LIGHT HORSE

The Great War

2nd Lieutenant Hugo Vivian Hope Throssell: 1915 – Gallipoli

227. THE AUSTRALIAN MACHINE-GUN CORPS

The Great War

(P) Sergeant Claude Charles Castleton: 5th Company: 1916 – France

Sergeant, The Hon. John James Dwyer, 4th Company: 1917 – Belgium

Lieutenant Edgar Thomas Towner, 2nd Company: 1918 – France

228. THE AUSTRALIAN INFANTRY CORPS

The Great War

Private Albert Jacka, (14th Victoria): 1915 – Gallipoli

Private Leonard Keyzor, (1st New South Wales): 1915 – Gallipoli

(P) Captain Alfred John Shout, (1st New South Wales): 1915 – Gallipoli

Lieutenant William John Symons, (7th Victoria): 1915 – Gallipoli

Lieutenant Frederick Harold Tubb, (7th Victoria): 1915 – Gallipoli

(P) Corporal Alexander Stewart Burton, (7th Victoria): 1915 – Gallipoli

Corporal William Dunstan, (7th Victoria): 1915 – Gallipoli

Private John Patrick Hamilton, (3rd New South Wales): 1915 – Gallipoli

Private William John Jackson, (17th New South Wales): 1915 – France

2nd Lieutenant Arthur Seaforth Blackburn, (10th South Australia & Western Australia): 1916 – France

Private Jack Leak, (9th Queensland): 1916 – France

(P) Private Thomas Cooke, (8th Victoria): 1916 – France

Private Martin O'Meara, (16th South Australia & Western Australia): 1916 – France

Captain Henry William Murray, (13th New South Wales): 1917 – France

(P) Captain Percy Herbert Cherry, (26th Queensland & Tasmania): 1917 – France

Private Jorgan Christian Jensen, (50th South Australia): 1917 – France

Captain John Ernest Newland, (12th South Australia): 1917 – France

Sergeant John Woods Whittle, (12th South Australia, Western Australia & Tasmania): 1917 – France

Private Thomas James Bede Kenny, (2nd New South Wales): 1917 – France

(P) Lieutentant Charles Pope, (11th Western Australia): 1917 – France

Corporal George Julian Howell, (1st New South Wales): 1917 – France

Lieutenant Rupert Vance Moon, (58th Victoria): 1917 – France

Captain Robert Cuthbert Grieve, (37th Victoria): 1917 – Belgium

Private John Carroll, (33rd New South Wales): 1917 – France

Private Reginald Roy Inwood, (10th South Australia): 1917 – Belgium

Lance-Corporal Walter Peeler, (3rd Pioneer): 1917 – Belgium

(P) 2nd Lieutenant Frederick Birks, (6th Victoria): 1917 – Belgium

(P) Private Patrick Joseph Bugden, (31st Queensland & Victoria): 1917 – Belgium

(P) Sergeant Lewis McGee, (40th Tasmania): 1917 – Belgium

(P) Captain Clarence Smith Jeffries, (34th New South Wales): 1917 – Belgium

Sergeant Stanley Robert McDougall, (47th Queensland): 1917 – France

Lieutenant Percy Valentine Storkey, (19th New South Wales): 1917 – France

Lieutenant Clifford William King Sadlier, (51st Victoria): 1918 – France

Sergeant William Ruthven, (22nd Victoria): 1918 – France

Corporal Philip Davey, (10th South Australia): 1918 – France

Lance-Corporal Thomas Leslie Axford, (16th South Australia & Western Australia): 1918 – France

Driver Henry Dalziel, (15th Queensland & Tasmania): 1918 – France

Act. Corporal Walter Ernest Brown, (20th New South Wales): 1918 – France

Lieutenant Albert Chalmers Borella, (26th Queensland & Tasmania): 1918 – France

(P) Lieutenant Alfred Edward Gaby, (28th Western Australia): 1918 – France

(P) Private Robert Matthew Beatham, (8th Victoria): 1918 – France

Sergeant Percy Clyde Statton, (40th Tasmania): 1918 – France

Lieutenant William Donovan Joynt, (8th Victoria): 1918 – France

Lieutenant Lawrence Dominic McCarthy, (16th South Australia & Western Australia): 1918 – France

Lance-Corporal Bernard Sidney Gordon, (41st Queensland): 1918 – France

Private George Cartwright, (33rd New South Wales): 1918 – France

Sergeant Albert David Lowerson, (21st Victoria): 1918 – France

Private William Matthew Currey, (53rd New South Wales): 1918 – France

(P) Private Robert Mactier, (23rd Victoria): 1918 – France

Corporal Arthur Charles Hall, (54th New South Wales): 1918 – France

(P) Private Alexander Henry Buckley, (54th New South Wales): 1918 – France

Lance-Corporal Lawrence Carthage Weathers, (43rd South Australia): 1918 – France

Sergeant Gerald Sexton, (13th New South Wales): 1918 – France
(Real name: Maurice Vincent Buckley)

Private James Park Woods, (48th South Australia): 1918 – France

Major Blair Anderson Wark, (32nd South Australia & Western Australia): 1918 – France

Private John Ryan, (55th New South Wales): 1918 – France

Lieutenant Joseph Maxwell, (18th New South Wales): 1918 – France

Lieutenant George Morby Ingram, (34th Victoria): 1918 – France

2nd World War

(P) Corporal John Hurst Edmondson (2/17th New South Wales): 1941 – Tobruk

Private James Heather Gordon, (31st Queensland & Victoria): 1941 – Syria

Lieutenant-Colonel Charles Groves Wright Anderson, (19th New South Wales) 1942 – Malaya

(P) Private Arthur Stanley Gurney, (48th South Australia): 1942 – Egypt

(P) Private Bruce Steel Kingsbury, (14th Victoria): 1942 – New Guinea

(P) Corporal John Alexander French, (9th Queensland): 1942 – New Guinea

(P) Sergeant William Henry Kibby, (48th South Australia): 1942 – Libya

(P) Private Percival Eric Gratwick, (48th South Australia): 1942 – Libya

Private Richard Kelliher, (25th Queensland): 1943 – New Guinea

Sergeant Thomas Currie Derrick, (48th South Australia): 1943 – New Guinea

Corporal Reginald Roy Rattey, (25th Queensland): 1945 – Solomon Islands

(P) Lieutenant Albert Chowne, (2nd New South Wales):

(P) Corporal John Bernard Mackay, (3rd Pioneer): 1945 – East Indies

Private Edward Kenna, (4th New SouthWales): 1945 – New Guinea

Private Leslie Thomas Starcevich, (43rd South Australia): 1945 – North Borneo

Private Frank John Partridge, (8th Victoria): 1945 – Solomon Islands

229. THE AUSTRALIAN ARMY TRAINING TEAM

Vietnam

(P) Warrant Officer Class II Kevin Arthur Wheatley: 1965 – Tra Bong

(P) Major Peter John Badcoe: 1967 – Huong Tru

Warrant Officer Class II Rayene Stewart Simpson: 1969 – Ben Het

Warrant Officer Class II Keith Payne: 1969 – Ben Het

230. THE ROYAL NEW ZEALAND AIR FORCE

2nd World War

Sergeant James Allen Ward: 1941 – Holland
(Serving with 75 Squadron, RAF.)

Squadron-Leader Leonard Henry Trent: 1943 – Holland
(Serving with 487 Squadron, RAF.)

(P) Flying-Officer Lloyd Allan Trigg: 1943 – Atlantic Ocean
(Serving with 200 Squadron, RAF. Coastal Command)

231. THE AUCKLAND MILITIA

New Zealand

Major Charles Heaphy: 1864 – Mangapiko River

232. 4th NEW ZEALAND CONTINGENT

South Africa (Boer)

Farrier-Major William James Hardman: 1901 – Cape Colony

233. NEW ZEALAND ENGINEERS

The Great War

(P) Sergeant Samuel Forsyth: 1918 – France
(Attached: 2nd Btn. Auckland Infantry Regiment)

234. NEW ZEALAND INFANTRY

The Great War

Corporal Cyril Royston Guyton Bassett: 1915 – Gallipoli
(New Zealand Divisional Signal Company)

(P) Sergeant Donald Forrester Brown: 1916 – France
(2nd Btn. Otago Infantry Regiment)

Lance-Corporal Samuel Frickleton: 1917 – Belgium
(3rd Btn. New Zealand Rifle Brigade)

Corporal Leslie Wilton Andrew: 1917 – France
(2nd Btn. Wellington Infantry Regiment)

Private Henry James Nicholas: 1917 – Belgium
(1st Btn. Canterbury Infantry Regiment)

(P) Sergeant Richard Charles Travis: 1918 – France
(Real name Dickson Cornelius Savage) (2nd Btn. Otago Infantry Regiment)

Sergeant Reginald Stanley Judson: 1918 – France
(1st Btn. Auckland Infantry Regiment)

Sergeant John Gilroy Grant: 1918 – France
(1st Btn. Wellington Infantry Regiment)

Sergeant Henry John Laurent: 1918 – France
(2nd Btn. New Zealand Rifle Brigade)

Private James Crichton: 1918 – France
(2nd Btn. Auckland Infantry Regiment)

2nd World War

Sergeant John Daniel Hinton: 1941 – Greece
(20th Wellington Btn. Canterbury Regiment)

Sergeant Alfred Clive Hulme: 1941 – Crete
(23rd Wellington Btn. Canterbury Regiment)

Lieutenant Charles Hazlett Upham: 1941 – Crete
(20th Wellington Btn. Canterbury Regiment)
(Lieutenant Upham later gained a bar to his VC: 1942 – Western Desert)

Sergeant Keith Elliott: 1942 – Western Desert
(22nd Wellington Btn. Canterbury Regiment)

(P) 2nd Lieutenant Moana Nui-a-Kiwa Ngarimu: 1943 – Tunisia
(28th Wellington Btn. Canterbury Regiment)

235. FIJIAN INFANTRY

2nd World War

(P) Corporal Sefanaia Sukanaivalu, 3rd Btn: 1944 – Solomon Islands

236. THE UNKNOWN WARRIOR OF THE UNITED STATES OF AMERICA

NOTES ON REORGANISATIONS

3 & 4: With a view to creating a British Army Air Arm an air battalion of the Royal Engineers was formed in 1911, and The Royal Flying Corps developed out of this in the following year. The RFC. was divided into a military and naval wing. The Royal Naval Air Service developed out of the naval wing of the RFC. and came into being in 1914. In 1918 personnel of the RFC. and the RNAS. merged to form the Royal Air Force. The RNAS. was revived in 1923 as The Fleet Air Arm.

5: In 1969 the 1st Royal Dragoons amalgamated with The Royal Horse Guards (The Blues), to form The Blues and Royals. The Blues and Royals and The Life Guards now form the Household Cavalry, which maintains cavalry squadrons for State occasions.

6 & 7: In 1969 these regiments amalgamated to form the 1st Queen's Dragoon Guards

8: In 1922 the 3rd Dragoon Guards (Prince of Wales's) and the 6th Dragoon Guards (Carabiniers) amalgamated to form the 3rd Carabiniers (Prince of Wales's Dragoon Guards). The 3rd Carabiniers and The Royal Scots Greys amalgamated in 1971 to form The Royal Scots Dragoon Guards (Carabiniers & Greys).

9 & 12: In 1922 these regiments amalgamated to form the 4th/7th Royal Dragoon Guards.

10 & 11: In 1922 these regiments amalgamated to form the 5th Royal Inniskilling Dragoon Guards.

12: In 1958 this regiment amalgamated with the 3rd King's Own Hussars to form The Queen's Own Hussars.

13 & 14: In 1958 these regiments amalgamated to form The Queen's Royal Irish Hussars.

15: In 1960 this regiment amalgamated with the 12th Royal Lancers (Prince of Wales's) to form the 9th/12th Royal Lancers (Prince of Wales's).

16 & 17: In 1969 these regiments amalgamated to form The Royal Hussars (Prince of Wales's Own).

18 & 19: In 1922 these regiments amalgamated to form the 13th/18th Royal Hussars (Queen Mary's Own).

20: In 1922 this regiment amalgamated with the 20th Hussars to form the 14th/20th King's Hussars.

21 & 22: In 1922 these regiments amalgamated to form the 15th/19th The King's Hussars.

23 & 24: In 1922 these regiments amalgamated to form the 16th/5th The Queen's Royal Lancers.

25 & 26: In 1922 these regiments amalgamated to form the 17th/21st Lancers (Duke of Cambridge's Own).

27 & 28: For security reasons the first British tank crews were known as The Heavy Branch, Machine Gun Corps, and in 1917 they became The Tank Corps, being granted the word 'Royal' in 1923. In 1928/29 the 11th Hussars and the 12th Lancers were converted into 'Cavalry Armoured Car Regiments'. In 1939 eighteen cavalry regiments and all units of The Royal Tank Corps were mechanised as The Royal

Armoured Corps. The Royal Tank Corps was later renamed The Royal Tank Regiment.

34: After 1860 the East India Company's Horse Artillery was absorbed into The Royal Regiment of Artillery.

36: After the Indian Mutiny the Bengal, Madras and Bombay Corps of Engineers were transferred to The Corps of Royal Engineers.

43 & 44: In 1959 these regiments amalgamated to form The Queen's Royal Surrey Regiment.

45 & 46: In 1961 these regiments amalgamated to form The Queen's Own Buffs, The Royal Kent Regiment.

43 to 48: In 1966 all these regiments amalgamated to form The Queen's Royal Regiment.

49 & 50: In 1959 these regiments amalgamated to form The King's Own Royal Border Regiment.

51 to 54: In 1968 all these regiments amalgamated to form The Royal Regiment of Fusiliers.

55 & 56: In 1958 these regiments amalgamated to form The King's Regiment (Manchester and Liverpool).

57 & 58: In 1959 these regiments amalgamated to form the 1st East Anglian Regiment (Royal Norfolk and Suffolk).

59 & 60: In 1960 these regiments amalgamated to form the 2nd East Anglian Regiment (Duchess of Gloucester's Own Royal Lincolnshire and Northamptonshire).

61 & 62: In 1958 these regiments amalgamated to form the 3rd East Anglian Regiment (Bedfordshire, Hertfordshire and Essex).

63: In 1964 this regiment was re-designated the 4th East Anglian Regiment.

57 to 63: In 1964 all these regiments amalgamated to form The Royal Anglian Regiment.

64 & 65: In 1958 these regiments amalgamated to form The Devonshire and Dorsetshire Regiment.

66 & 67: In 1959 these regiments amalgamated to form The Somerset and Cornwall Light Infantry.

66 to 70: In 1968 all these regiments amalgamated to form The Light Infantry.

71 & 72: In 1958 these regiments amalgamated to form The Prince of Wales's Own Regiment of Yorkshire.

74 & 75: In 1959 these regiments amalgamated to form The Royal Highland Fusiliers (Princess Margaret's Own Glasgow and Ayrshire Regiment.)

78 & 79: In 1969 these regiments amalgamated to form The Royal Regiment Of Wales (24th/41st Foot).

81: In 1968 this regiment was disbanded to avoid amalgamation.

82 to 84: In 1968 all these regiments amalgamated to form The Royal Irish Rangers (27th Inniskilling, 83rd/87th).

86 & 87: In 1970 these regiments amalgamated to form The Worcestershire and Sherwood Foresters Regiment (29th/45th Foot).

88 & 89: In 1958 these regiments amalgamated to form The Lancashire Regiment (Prince of Wales's Volunteers).

88 to 90: In 1970 these regiments amalgamated to form The Queen's Lancashire Regiment.

93 & 94: In 1959 these regiments amalgamated to form The Staffordshire Regiment (The Prince of Wales's).

96 & 97: In 1959 these regiments amalgamated to form The Duke of Edinburgh's Royal Regiment (Berkshire and Wiltshire).

98: In 1968 this regiment disbanded to avoid amalgamation.

99 & 100: In 1961 these regiments amalgamated to form the Queen's Own Highlanders (Seaforth and Camerons).

104 to 111: When the Indian Continent was partitioned in 1947 the 2nd 6th, 7th and 10th Gurkha Rifles were assigned to the British Army, and the other six went to the Indian Army.

112: In 1958 this regiment was re-designated the 1st Royal Green Jackets.

113: In 1958 this regiment was re-designated the 2nd Royal Green Jackets.

114: In 1958 this regiment was re-designated the 3rd Royal Green Jackets.

112 to 114: In 1966 these regiments amalgamated to form The Royal Green Jackets (43rd/52nd, K.R.R.C. & Rifle Brigade).

116 to 120: In 1922 these regiments were disbanded on the formation of The Irish Free State.

121: In 1937 this regiment ceased to exist and the units which composed it were linked with line regiments.

122: During the South African War, 1899-1902, The London Scottish served with its parent regular regiment, The Gordon Highlanders. In 1908 it joined the territorial forces and took the title 14th (Co. of London) Btn. The London Regiment. In 1937 it was linked with The Gordon Highlanders.

124: In 1927 this regiment was disbanded, but was revived during the 2nd World War as The Caribbean Regiment. The Caribbean Regiment was disbanded in 1947, but its Jamaica and Barbados units survived.

126 to 128: A Land Transport Corps was formed during the Crimean War in 1855, which was merged with The Military Train in 1856. This in turn became The Army Service Corps in 1870, which in 1877 was divided into The Commissariat and Transport Corps and The Ordnance Store Branch. These became separate corps in 1880. In 1889 officers and men of The Commissariat and Transport Corps were amalgamated to form the 2nd Army Service Corps. The Royal Army Ordnance Corps has now taken over the A.S.C. provision of supplies, and The Royal Corps Of Transport its transport function.

128 to 131: Before The Medical Staff Corps was formed in 1855 during the Crimean War, medical services were organised by a Surgeon employed by the regiment to run a

field hospital, which was staffed by soldiers of the regiment that the hospital was set up to care for. In 1857 the Medical Staff Corps became The Army Hospital Corps, which was eventually officered by the Army Medical Corps, and in 1884 the doctors were formed into the Medical Staff Department. Many units continued to appoint their own doctors until The Royal Army Medical Corps came into being in 1898.

133: Later 21st Prince Albert Victor's Own Cavalry (Frontier Force) Daly's Horse.

134: Later 22nd Sam Brown's Cavalry (Frontier Force).

135: Later 32nd Lancers.

136: Later 33rd Queen Victoria's Own Light Cavalry.

138: Later 6th King Edward's Own Cavalry.

140: Later 14th Lancers (The Scind Horse).

144: Later 2nd Queen Victoria's Own Rajput Light Infantry.

147: Later 4th Prince Albert Victor's Own Rajputs.

154: Later 11th Rajputs.

158: Later 13th Rajputs (The Shekhawati Regiment).

162: Later 79th Carnatic Infantry.

163: Later 120th Rajputana Infantry.

164: Later 124th Duchess of Connaught's Own Baluchistan Infantry.

165: Later 125th Napier's Rifles.

166: Later 26th Punjabis.

168: Later 37th Dogras.

171: Later 46th Punjabis.

177: Later 66th Punjabis.

178: Later 72nd Punjabis.

INDEX

The Crimean War

Ablett, A	37	Dixon, MC	34	Lendrim, WJ.	36
Alexander, J.	81	Dowell, GD	2	Lennox, WO.	36
Arthur, T.	34	Dunn, AR.	17	Lindsay, RJ.	39
Beach, T.	50	Elphinstone, HC.	36	Lucas, CD.	1
Bell, EWD.	77	Elton, FC.	50	Lumley, CH.	46
Berryman, J.	25	Esmonde, T.	116	Lyons, J.	73
Bourchier, CT.	114	Evans, S.	73	McCorrie, C.	48
Bradshaw, J.	114	Farrell, J.	25	McDermond, J.	90
Buckley, CW.	1	Gardiner, G.	48	McDonald, H.	36
Burgoyne, JT.	1	Goodlake, GL.	37	McGregor, R.	114
Byrne, J.	70	Gorman, J	1	McKechnie, J.	39
Bythesea, J.	1	Grady, T.	49	McWheeney, W.	62
Cambridge, D.	34	Graham, G.	36	Madden, A.	79
Clifford, HH.	114	Grieve, J.	8	Malone, J.	18
Coffey, W.	50	Hales, TE.	53	Maude, FF.	45
Coleman, J.	46	Hamilton, T.De.C.	70	Miller, F.	34
Commerell, JE.	1	Henry, A.	34	Mouat, J.	11
Connors, J.	45	Hewett, WNW.	1	Moynihan, A.	81
Conolly, JA.	96	Hope, W.	53	Norman, W.	53
Cooper, H.	1	Hughes, M.	53	O'Connor, L.	77
Craig, J.	39	Humpston, R.	114	Owens, J.	96
Cuninghame, WJM.	114	Ingouville, G.	1	Palmer, A.	37
Curtis, H.	1	Johnstone, W.	1	Park, J.	48
Daniel, E.St.J.	1	Jones, HM.	53	Parkes, S.	13
Davis, G.	34	Kellaway, J.	1	Peel, W.	1
Day, GF.	1	Knox, JS.	39	Percy, HHM.	37
Dickson, C	34	Leitch, P.	36	Perie, J.	36

Prettyjohn, J.	2	Russell, C.	37	Symons, G.	34
Prosser, J.	42	Scholefield, M	1	Taylor, J.	1
Raby, HJ.	1	Sheppard, J.	1	Teesdale, CC.	34
Ramage, H.	8	Shields, R.	77	Trewavas, J.	1
Reeves, T.	1	Sims, JJ.	50	Walker, M.	88
Reynolds, W.	39	Smith, P.	63	Walters, G.	96
Rickard, WT.	1	Stanlack, W.	37	Wheatley, F.	114
Robarts, J.	1	Strong, G.	37	Wilkinson, T.	2
Ross, J.	36	Sullivan, J.	1	Wooden, C.	25
Rowlands, HH.	79	Sylvester, WHT.	77	Wright, A.	48

The Indian Mutiny

Addison, H.	112	Buckley, J.	183	Davis, J.	95
Aikman, FR.	147	Butler, TA.	119	Dempsey, D.	59
Aitken, RHM.	158	Byrne, J.	83	Diamond, B.	34
Anderson, C.	7	Cadell, T.	119	Divane, J.	113
Anson, AHA.	98	Cafe, WM.	174	Donohoe, P.	15
Baker, CG.	184	Cameron, AS.	99	Dowling. W.	67
Bambrick, V.	113	Carlin. P.	66	Duffy, T.	120
Bankes, WGM.	12	Champion, J.	14	Dunley, J.	102
Blair, J.	135	Chicken, GB.	1	Dynon, D.	69
Blair, R.	7	Clogstoun, HM.	162	Farquharson, FEH.	95
Bogle, A.C.	99	Cochrane, HS.	83	Ffrench, AK.	69
Boulger, A.	98	Connolly. W.	34	FitzGerald, R.	34
Bradshaw, W.	81	Cook, W.	95	Flinn, T.	94
Brennan, J.	34	Coghlan, C.	101	Forrest, G.	185
Brown, FDM.	119	Crowe, JPH.	99	Fraser, CC.	12
Browne, HG.	67	Cubitt, WG.	158	Freeman, J.	15
Browne, SJ.	171	Daunt, JCC.	154	Gardner, W.	95

106

Garvin, S.	113	Innes, JJ.McL.	36	McQuirt, B.	87
Gill, P.	159	Irwin, C.	69	Mahoney, P.	120
Goat, W.	15	Jarrett, HCT.	166	Mangles, RL.	187
Goodfellow, CA.	36	Jee, J.	99	Maude, FC.	34
Gough, CJS.	137	Jennings, E.	34	Mayo, A.	1
Gough, HH.	22	Jerome, HE.	83	Millar, D.	95
Graham, P.	81	Jones, AS.	15	Miller, J.	183
Grant, P.	102	Kavanagh, TH.	187	Monaghan, T.	7
Grant, R.	51	Keatinge, RH.	34	Monger, G.	77
Green, P.	101	Kells, R.	15	Morley, S.	126
Guise, JG.	81	Kenny, J.	69	Munro, J.	102
Hackett, TB	77	Kerr, WA.	164	Murphy, M.	126
Hall, W.	1	Kirk, J.	59	Mylott, WP.	98
Hancock, T.	15	Lambert, G.	98	Napier, W.	66
Harington, HE.	34	Laughnan, T.	34	Nash, W.	114
Harrison, J.	1	Lawrence, SH.	67	Newell, R.	15
Hartigan, H.	15	Leith, J.	20	Olpherts, W.	34
Havelock, HM.	59	Lyster, HH.	178	Oxenham, W.	67
Hawkes, D.	114	McBean, W.	102	Park, J.	34
Hawthorne, R.	112	McDonell, WF.	187	Paton, J.	102
Heathcote, AS.	113	McGovern, J.	119	Pearson, James	83
Heneage, CW.	14	McGuire, J.	119	Pearson, John	14
Hill, S.	81	McHale, P.	51	Phillips, EAL.	154
Hills, J.	34	McInnes, H.	34	Prendergast, HND.	36
Hollis, G.	14	Mackay, D.	102	Probyn, DM.	134
Hollowell, J.	99	MacManus, P.	51	Purcell, J.	15
Holmes, J.	98	McMaster, VM.	99	Pye, C.	69
Home, AD.	81	MacPherson, HT.	99	Raynor, W.	185
Home, DC.	36	MacPherson, S.	99	Reade, HT.	85

Rennie, W.	81	Shebbeare, RH.	176	Tombs, H.	34
Renny, GA.	34	Simpson, J.	95	Travers, J.	144
Richardson, G.	50	Sinnott, J.	98	Turner, S.	113
Roberts, FS.	34	Sleavon, M.	36	Tytler, JA.	177
Roberts, JR.	15	Smith, H.	112	Wadeson, R.	101
Robinson, E.	1	Smith, J.	36	Waller, G.	113
Roddy, P.	181	Smith, John	120	Waller, WFF.	165
Rodgers, G.	75	Spence, D.	15	Ward, H.	99
Rosamund, M.	168	Spence, E.	95	Ward, J.	14
Rushe, D.	15	Stewart, WGD	102	Watson, J.	133
Ryan, J.	120	Sutton, W.	113	Whirlpool, F.	118
Ryan, M.	119	Thackeray, ET	36	Wilmot, H.	114
Salkeld, P.	36	Thomas, J.	34	Wood, HE.	25
Salmon, N.	1	Thompson, A.	95	Young, TJ.	1
Shaw, S.	114	Thompson, J.	113		

New Zealand, Afghanistan and The Zulu War (NZ, A and ZW)

Adams, JW. (A)	186	Cook, J. (A)	132	Hook, A. (ZW)	78
Allan, WN. (ZW)	78	Creagh, O. (A)	132	Jones, R. (ZW)	78
Ashford, TE. (A)	53	Cunyngham, WHD. (A)	101	Jones, W. (ZW)	78
Beresford, WdelaP (ZW)	15	Dalton, JL. (ZW)	127	Leach, EP. (A)	36
Booth, AC. (ZW)	93	D'Arcy, HCD. (ZW)	189	Leet, WK. (ZW)	66
Bromhead, G.(ZW)	78	Down, JT. (NZ)	48	Lucas, J. (NZ)	89
Browne, ES. (ZW)	78	Fowler, EJ. (ZW)	81	Lysons, H. (ZW)	81
Buller, RH. (ZW)	113	Hamilton, WRP. (A)	132	MacKenna, E. (NZ)	98
Chard, JRM. (ZW)	36	Hammond, AG. (A)	132	McNeill, JC. (NZ)	47
Chase, W St. L (A)	132	Hart, RC. (A)	36	Manley, WG. (NZ)	34
Coghill, NJA (ZW)	78	Heaphy, C. (NZ)	231	Melvill, T. (ZW)	78
Collis, J. (A)	34	Hitch, F. (ZW)	78	Mitchell, S. (NZ)	1

Mullane, P. (A)	34	Ryan, J. (NZ)	98	Stagpoole, D. (NZ)	48
Murray, J. (NZ)	70	Sartorius, EH. (A)	88	Temple, W. (NZ)	34
Odgers, W. (NZ)	1	Schiess, FC. (ZW)	190	Vousden, WJ. (A)	132
O'Toole, E. (ZW)	189	Sellar, G. (A)	99	Wassall, S. (ZW)	93
Pickard, AF. (NZ)	34	Shaw, H. (NZ)	116	White, GS. (A)	101
Reynolds. JH. (ZW)	130	Smith, A. (NZ)	34	Williams, J. (ZW)	78

Others (Pre-Great War)

Adams, RB.	132	De Montmorency, RHLJ.	26	Harding, I.	1
Aylmer, FJ.	36	Doogan, J.	6	Hartley, EB.	191
Baxter, FW.	195	Douglas, CM.	78	Henderson, HS.	195
Bell, D.	78	Dundas, J.	36	Hill, AR.	60
Bell, MS.	36	Edwards, WMM.	75	Hinckley, G.	1
Bergin, J.	91	Edwards, T.	95	Hodge, S.	124
Boisragon, GH.	132	Farmer, JJ.	129	Kenna, PA.	26
Boyes, DG.	1	Fincastle, Viscount	23	Lane, T.	92
Brown, P.	191	Findlater, G.	101	Lawson, E.	101
Burslem, N.	92	Fitzgibbon, A.	182	Lenon, EH.	92
Byrne, T.	26	Fitzpatrick, F.	117	Le Quesne, FG.	130
Carter, HA.	132	Flawn, T.	117	Lloyd, OEP.	130
Channer, GN.	132	Fosbury, GV.	145	McClean, HLS.	132
Chaplin, JW.	92	Gifford, The Lord	78	McCrea, JF.	192
Cobbe, AS.	132	Gordon, WJ.	124	McDougall, J.	62
Colvin, JMC.	36	Gough, JE.	114	McGaw, S.	95
Cooper, J.	78	Grant, CJW.	132	Macintyre, D.	132
Corbett, F.	113	Grant, JD.	132	Mackenzie, J.	99
Costello, EW.	132	Griffiths, W.	78	Magner, M.	91
Crimmin, J.	182	Guy, BJD.	1	Maillard, WJ.	1
Danaher, J.	193	Halliday, LST.	2	Malcolmson, JG.	136

Marling, PS.	113	Pride, T.	1	Smith, J.M.	132
Marshall, W.	22	Ridgeway, RK.	132	Smyth, NM.	7
Mellis, CJ.	132	Rolland, GM.	132	Trevor, WS.	36
Moore, AT.	136	Rogers, RM.	62	Vickery, S.	65
Moore, HG.	117	Ruthven, AGA H-	75	Walker, WG.	132
Murphy, T.	78	Sartorius, RW.	138	Watson, TC.	36
Murray, J.	117	Scott, A.	132	Whitchurch, HF.	182
Nesbitt, RC.	194	Scott, RG.	191	Wilson, AK.	1
O'Hea, T.	114	Seeley, WHH.	1	Wood, JA.	163
Osborne, J.	60	Smith, CL.	67	Wright, WD.	43
Pennell, HS.	87	Smith, FA.	112		
Pitcher, HW.	146	Smith, J.	45		

South Africa (Boer)

Albrecht, H.	200	Crean, TJ.	200	Hardham, WJ.	232
Atkinson, A.	73	Curtis, AE.	44	Heaton, W.	55
Babtie, W.	131	Davies, LAE P-	113	Holland, EJG.	209
Barry, J.	116	Douglas, HEM.	131	Hornby, EJ P-	34
Bees, W.	87	Doxat, AC.	33	House, W.	96
Beet, HC.	87	Dugdale, FB.	24	Howse, NR.	223
Bell, FW.	224	Durrant, E.	114	Ind, AE.	34
Bisdee, JH.	222	Engleheart, HW.	16	Indkson, ET.	131
Bradley, FH.	34	English, W.J.	31	Johnston, R.	200
Brown, ED.	20	Farmer, D.	100	Jones, C M-	71
Clements, JJ.	197	Firth, J.	91	Jones, RJTD.	36
Cockburn, HZC.	209	FitzClarence, C.	53	Kennedy, CT.	75
Congreve, WN.	114	Glasock, HH.	34	Kirby, FH.	36
Coulson, GHB.	80	Gordon, WE.	101	Knight, HJ.	55
Crandon, HG.	19	Hampton, H.	55	Lawrence, BT.	25

Leake, A M- + bar	131 + 199	Norwood, J.	10	Rogers, J.	199
Lodge, I.	34	Nurse, GE.	34	Schofield, HN.	34
Mackay, JF.	101	Parker, CEH.	34	Scott, R.	56
Martineau, HR.	196	Parsons, FN.	62	Shaul, JDF.	75
Masterson, JEI.	64	Pitts, J.	56	Rowse, EB.	101
Maxwell, FA.	132	Ramsden, HE.	196	Traynor, WB.	71
Maygar, LC.	225	Ravenhill, G.	74	Turner, REW.	209
Meiklejohn, MFM.	101	Reed, HL.	34	Ward, C.	68
Milbanke, JP.	16	Richardson, AHL.	210	Wylly, GGE.	222
Mullins, CH.	200	Roberts, FHS.	113	Young, A.	198
Nickerson, WHS.	131	Robertson, W.	101	Younger, DR.	101

The Great War

Ackroyd, H.	131	Badlu Singh	140	Bell, DS.	73
Acton, A.	50	Ball, A.	87	Bell, ENF.	82
Addison, WRF.	125	Bamford, E.	2	Bellew, ED.	216
Adlam, TE.	61	Barber, E.	37	Bennett, EP.	86
Agar, AWS.	1	Barker, WG.	4	Bent, PE.	63
Alexander, EW.	34	Barratt, T.	93	Bent, SJ.	88
Algie, WL.	216	Barrett, JC.	63	Bingham, EBS.	1
Allen, WB.	131	Barron, CF.	216	Birks, F.	228
Amey, W.	52	Barter, F.	77	Bishop, WA.	215
Anderson, W.	73	Bassett, CRG.	234	Bissett, WD.	102
Anderson, WH.	75	Baxter, EF.	55	Blackburn, AS.	228
Andrew, LW.	234	Beak, DMW.	1	Bloomfield, WA.	201
Angus, W.	75	Beale, EF.	73	Bonner, CG.	1
Archibald, A.	36	Beatham, RM.	228	Booth, FC.	203
Auten, H.	1	Beesley, W.	114	Borella, AC.	228
Axford, TL.	228	Belcher, DW.	121	Borton, AD.	121

Boughey, SHP.	74	Bushell, C.	43	Clare, GW.	24
Boulter, WE.	60	Butler, JFP.	113	Clarke, J.	54
Bourke, RRl.	1	Butler, WB.	71	Clarke, L.	216
Boyle, EC.	1	Bye, RJ.	41	Cloutman, BM.	36
Bradbury, EK.	34	Caffrey, J.	98	Coffin, C.	36
Bradford, GN.	1	Cairns, H,	216	Colley, HJ.	54
Bradford, RB.	70	Caldwell, T.	74	Collin, JH.	49
Brereton, AP.	216	Calvert, L.	68	Collins, J.	77
Brilliant, J.	216	Campbell, FW.	216	Cottman, WH.	94
Brodie, WL.	75	Campbell, G.	1	Columbine, HG.	27
Bromley, C.	54	Campbell, JV.	38	Colvin, H.	76
Brooke, JAO.	101	Carless, JH.	1	Combe, RG.	216
Brooks, E.	112	Carmichael, J.	94	Congreve, W. La.T.	114
Brooks, O.	38	Carpenter, AFB.	1	Cooke, T.	228
Brown, DF.	234	Carroll, J.	228	Cookson, EC.	1
Brown, H.	216	Carter, NV.	47	Cooper, E.	113
Brown, WE.	228	Cartwright, G.	228	Cooper, NB E-	53
Bruce, WA. McC.	175	Cassidy, BM.	54	Coppins, FG.	216
Bryan, T.	51	Castleton, CC.	227	Cornwell, JT.	1
Buchan, JC.	102	Cates, GE.	114	Cosgrove, W.	119
Buchanan, A.	78	Cather, G. St.G.S.	84	Cotter, WR.	45
Buckingham, W.	63	Cator, H.	44	Counter, JT.	55
Buckley, AH.	228	Chafer, GW.	72	Coury, GG.	89
Buckley, MV.	228	Chatta Singh.	151	Coverdale, CH.	56
Bugden, PJ.	228	Chavasse, NG. + bar	131	Cowley, CH.	1
Burges, D.	85	Cherry, PH.	228	Cox, CA.	61
Burman, WF.	114	Christian, H.	49	Craig, JM.	74
Burt, AA.	123	Christie, JA.	121	Crichton, J.	234
Burton, AS.	228	Clamp, W.	73	Crisp, T.	1

Croak, JB.	216	Dimmer, JHS.	113	Evans, LP.	95
Cross, AH.	27	Dinesen, T.	216	Faulds, WF.	202
Crowe, JJ.	86	Dobson, CG.	1	Fergusson, TR. C-	60
Cruickshank, RE.	122	Dobson, FW.	38	Finch, NA.	2
Crutchley, VAC.	1	Dorrell, GT.	34	Findlay, G.de.CE.	36
Cunningham, J. (Pte)	72	Dougall, ES.	34	Finlay, D.	95
Cunningham, J. (Corp)	118	Downie, R.	120	Firman, HOB.	1
Currey, WM.	228	Doyle, M.	119	Fisher, F.	216
Curtis, HA.	120	Drain, JHC.	34	Flowerdew, GM.	210
Dalziel, H.	228	Drake, AG.	114	Forshaw, WT.	56
Dancox, FG.	86	Dresser, T.	73	Forsyth, S.	233
Daniels, H.	114	Drewry, GL.	1	Foss, CC.	61
Dartnel, WT.	53	Drummond, GH.	1	Foster, E.	44
Darwan Sing Negi	169	Duffy, J.	82	Freyburg, BC.	43
Davey, P.	228	Dunkley, B. B-	54	Frickleton, S.	234
Davies, JJ.	77	Dunsire, R.	42	Frisby, CH.	38
Davies, JL.	77	Dunstan, W.	228	Fuller, WD.	37
Davies JT.	89	Dunville, JS.	5	Fuller, W.	79
Davies, RB.	3	Dwyer, E.	44	Fynn, JH.	78
Dawson, JL.	36	Dwyer, JJ.	227	Gaby, AE.	228
Day, SJ.	58	Edwards, A.	99	Garforth, CE.	21
Daykins, JB.	98	Edwards, FJ.	48	Greary, BH.	44
Dean, DJ.	46	Edwards, W.	68	Gee, R.	53
Dean, PT,	1	Egerton, EA.	87	Gill, A.	113
Dease, MJ.	53	Elcock, RE.	42	Gobar Sing Negi	169
de Pass, FA	142	Elstob, W.	56	Gobind Singh	141
de Wiart, AC.	9	Emerson, JS.	82	Godley, SF.	53
De Wind, E.	83	Erskine, J.	81	Good, HJ.	216
Diarmid, AMC.McR-	48	Evans, WJG.	56	Gordon, BS.	228

Gorle, RV.	34	Hardy, TB.	125	Horlock, EG.	34
Gort, Viscount	37	Harris, TJ.	46	Horsfall, BA.	88
Gosling, W.	34	Harrison, AL.	1	Howell, GJ.	228
Gourley, CE.	34	Harrison, J.	72	Hudson, CE.	87
Graham, JRN.	102	Harvey, FJW.	2	Huffam, JP.	91
Grant, JG.	234	Harvey, FMW.	210	Hughes, T.	117
Greaves, F.	87	Harvey, J.	121	Hull, C.	26
Green, JL.	131	Harvey, N.	82	Hunter, DF.	75
Greenwood, H.	68	Harvey, S.	98	Hutcheson, BS.	218
Gregg, MF.	216	Hawker, LG.	36	Hutchinson, J.	54
Gregg, W.	114	Hayward, RFJ.	97	Hutt, A.	52
Grenfell, FO.	15	Heaviside, M.	70	Ingram, GM.	228
Gribble, JR.	52	Hedges, FW.	61	Insall, GSM.	4
Grieve, RC.	228	Henderson, A.	102	Inwood, RR.	228
Grimbaldeston, WH.	80	Henderson, EED.	94	Jacka, A.	228
Grimshaw, JE.	54	Herring, AC.	128	Jackson, H.	72
Grogan, GW.St.G.	86	Hewitson, J.	49	Jackson, TN.	38
Hackett, W.	36	Hewitt, DGW.	92	Jackson, WJ.	228
Haine, RL.	35	Hewitt, WH.	202	James, H.	86
Hall, AC.	228	Hill, A.	77	James, MA.	85
Hall, FW.	216	Hirsch, DP.	73	Jarratt, G.	53
Halliwall, J.	54	Hobson, F.	216	Jarvis, CA.	36
Hallowes, RP.	48	Hogan, J.	56	Jeffries, CS.	228
Halton, A.	49	Holbrook, ND.	1	Jensen, JC.	228
Hamilton, AF. D-	100	Holland, JV.	118	Jerrard, A.	4
Hamilton, JB	75	Holmes, FW.	68	Johnson, DG.	78
Hamilton, JP.	228	Holmes, TW.	215	Johnson, FH.	36
Hanna, RH.	216	Holmes, WE.	37	Johnson, J.	51
Hansen, PH.	59	Honey, SL	216	Johnson, WH.	36

Name	Page	Name	Page	Name	Page
Johnston, WH.	87	Knox, CL.	36	MacDowell, TW.	216
Jones, D.	55	Konowal, F.	216	McFadzean, WF.	83
Jones, LW.	1	Kulbir Thapa	105	McGee, L.	228
Jones, RBB.	90	Lafone, AM.	33	McGregor, DS.	42
Jones, TA.	76	Laidlaw, D.	80	MacGregor, J.	215
Jotham, E.	172	Lala.	170	McGuffie, L.	80
Joynt, WD.	228	Lascelles, AM.	70	McIntosh, GI.	101
Judson, RS.	234	Lauder, DR.	74	MacIntyre, DL.	102
Kaeble, J.	216	Laurent, HJ.	234	McIver, H.	42
Karanbahadur Rana	105	Leach, J.	56	McKean, GB.	216
Kelly, H.	91	Leak, J.	228	McKenzie, AE.	1
Kelly, J. S-	57	Leake, A. M- + Bar	131&199	McKenzie, H.	212
Keneally, W.	54	Learmonth, OM.	216	MacKenzie, James	39
Kennedy, WH. C-	216	Lester, F.	54	Mackintosh, D.	99
Kenny, HE.	90	Lewis, AL.	60	McLeod, AA.	4
Kenny, T.	70	Lewis, HW.	79	McNair, EA.	47
Kenny, TJB.	228	Liddell, JA.	102	McNally, W.	73
Kenny, W.	101	Lister, J.	54	McNamara, FH.	220
Ker, AE.	101	Loosemoore, A.	91	McNamara, J.	44
Kerr, GF.	216	Lowerson, AD.	228	McNess, F.	39
Kerr, JC.	216	Luke, F.	34	McPhie, J.	36
Keysor, L.	228	Lumsden, FW.	2	Mactier, R.	228
Keyworth, LJ.	121	Lyall, GT.	216	Maling, GA.	131
Khudadad Khan	180	Lynn, J.	54	Malleson, W.St.A.	1
Kilby, AFG.	93	AcAulay, J.	39	Mannock, E.	4
Kinross, CJ.	216	McBeath, R.	99	Mariner, W.	113
Kirk, James	56	McCarthy, LD.	228	Marshall, JN.	40
Knight, AG.	216	McCudden, JTB.	4	Martin, CG.	36
Knight, AJ.	121	McDougall, SR.	228	Masters. RG.	128

Maufe, THB.	34	Mullin, GH.	216	Pearse, SG.	53
Maxwell, J.	228	Murray, HW.	228	Peck, CW.	216
May, H.	81	Myles, EK.	79	Peeler, W.	228
Mayson, TF.	49	Nasmith, ME.	1	Phillips, RE.	52
Meekosha, S.	71	Neame, P.	36	Pitcher, EH.	1
Meikle, J.	99	Needham, S.	61	Pollard, AO.	35
Mellish, EN.	125	Neeley, T.	49	Pollock, JD.	100
Melvin, C.	95	Nelson, D.	34	Pooll, AHH. B-	119
Merrifield, W.	216	Newland, JE.	228	Pope, C.	228
Metcalf, WH.	216	Nicholas, HJ.	234	Potts, FW.	30
Miles, FG.	85	Noble, CR.	114	Poutter, A.	91
Miller, J	49	Nunney, CJP.	216	Procter, AH.	55
Mills, W.	56	Ockenden, J.	120	Proctor, AFW. B-	4
Milne, WJ.	216	O'Kelly, CPJ.	216	Prowse, G.	1
Miner, HGB.	216	O'Leary, M.	40	Pryce, TT.	37
Mir Dast	173	O'Meara, M.	228	Quigg, R.	83
Mitchell, CN.	214	O'Neill, J.	118	Ranken, HS.	131
Moffatt, M	118	Onions, G.	64	Ratcliffe, W.	89
Molyneux, J.	53	Ormsby, JW.	68	Rayfield, WL.	216
Moon, RB.	228	O'Rourke, MJ.	216	Raynes, JC.	34
Moor, GRD.	92	O'Sullivan, GR.	82	Read, AM.	60
Moore, MSS.	92	Palmer, FW.	53	Readitt, J.	89
Moorhouse, WB. R-	4	Parker, WR.	2	Rees, I.	78
Morrow, R.	84	Parslow, FD.	1	Rees, LWB.	34
Mott, EJ.	50	Parsons, HF.	85	Reid, OA.	55
Mottershead, T.	4	Paton, GHT.	37	Rendle, TE.	67
Mountain, A.	71	Pattison, JG.	216	Reynolds. D.	34
Moyney, J.	40	Peachment, GS.	113	Reynolds. H.	42
Mugford, HS.	27	Pearkes, GR.	215	Rhodes, JH.	37

Richards, AJ.	54	Sandes, AJT. F-	44	Statton, Pc.	228
Richardson JC.	216	Sandford, RD.	1	Steele, GC.	1
Ricketts, T.	219	Saunders,f AF.	58	Steele, T.	99
Riggs, FC.	98	Sayer, JW.	43	Stone, CE.	34
Ripley, J.	95	Schofield, J.	54	Stone, WN.	53
Ritchie, HP.	1	Scrimger, FAC.	218	Storkey, PV.	228
Ritchie, WP.	99	Seaman, E.	82	Strachan, H.	211
Rivers, J.	87	Sewell, CH.	46	Stringer, GA.	56
Roberts, FC.	86	Sexton, G. (see MV. Buckley)		Stuart, RN.	1
Robertson, CG.	53	Shahamad Khan	179	Stubbs, FE.	54
Robertson, C.	43	Shand, SW. L-	73	Sullivan, AP.	53
Robertson, J. F-	50	Shankland, R.	216	Sykes, E.	51
Robertson, JP.	216	Sharpe, CR.	59	Symons. WJ.	228
Robinson, EG.	1	Shepherd, AE.	113	Tait, JE.	216
Robinson, WL	86	Short, W.	73	Tandey, H.	91
Robson, HH.	42	Shout, AJ.	228	Thomas, John	94
Rochfort, GA. B-	39	Simpson, WE.	59	Throssell, HVH.	226
Room, FG.	116	Sifton, EW.	216	Tisdall, AW.StC.	1
Roupell, GRP.	44	Sinton, JA.	182	Tollerton, R.	100
Russell, J. F-	131	Skinner, J.	80	Tombs, JH.	55
Rutherford, CS.	215	Smith, AV.	88	Towers, J.	81
Ruthven, W.	228	Smith, AB.	1	Towner, ET.	227
Ryan, J.	228	Smith, E.	54	Toye, AM.	48
Ryder, RE.	48	Smith, I.	56	Train, CW.	122
Sadlier, CWR.	228	Smith, James	50	Travis, RC.	234
Sage, TH.	66	Smyth, JG.	159	Tubb, FH.	228
Samson, G.McK.	1	Somers, J.	82	Turnbull, JY.	75
Sanders, G.	71	Spackman, CE.	50	Turner, AB.	96
Sanders, WE.	1	Spall, R.	216	Turrall, TG.	86

117

Unwin, E.	1	Weathers, LC.	228	Williams, WC.	1
Upton, J.	87	Welch, J.	96	Willis, RR.	54
Vallentin, JF.	93	Wells, H.	47	Wilson, G.	75
Vann, BW.	87	Wells, JS. C-	61	Wood, HB.	39
Veale, TWH.	64	West, FMF.	4	Wood, W.	51
Vickers, A.	52	West. RA.	32	Woodall, JE.	114
Vickers,CG.	87	Wheeler, GC.	110	Woodcock, T.	40
Wain, RWL.	28	Wheeler, GGM.	139	Woodroffe, SC.	114
Walford, GN.	34	White, A.	78	Woods, JP.	228
Wallace, STD.	34	White, ACT.	73	Woolley, GH.	121
Waller, H.	68	White, GS.	1	Wright, T.	36
Ware, SW.	99	White, J.	49	Wyatt, GH.	38
Waring, W.	77	White, WA.	27	Wylie, CHM. D-	77
Wark, BA.	228	Whitfield, H.	69	Yate, CAL.	68
Warneford, RAJ.	3	Whitham, T.	38	Yovens, F.	70
Warner, E.	61	Whittle, JW.	228	Youll, JS.	51
Waters, AHS.	36	Wilcox, A.	112	Young, FE.	123
Watson, OCS.	68	Wilkinson, AR.	56	Young, JF.	216
Watt, J.	1	Wilkinson, TOL.	90	Young, T.	70
Weale, H.	77	Williams, JH.	78	Young, W.	88
Wearne, FB.	62	Williams, W.	1	Zengel, RL.	216

2nd World War

Aaron, AL.	4	Anderson, E.	72	Bates, S.	57
Abdul Hafiz	152	Anderson, JT. McK-	102	Bazalgette, IW.	4
Agansingh Rai	106	Andrews, HM. E-	88	Beattie, SH.	1
Ali Haidar	157	Annand, AW.	70	Beeley, J.	113
Allmand, M.	29	Barton, CJ.	4	Bhanbhagta Gurung	104
Anderson, CGW.	228	Baskeyfield, JD.	93	Bhandari Ram	153

Blaker, FG.	75	Fegen, ESF.	1	Horwood, AG.	43
Brunt, JHC.	87	Foote, HRB.	28	Hulme, AC.	234
Burton, RH.	91	Foote, JW.	217	Hunter, TP.	2
Cain, RH.	51	Fraser, IE.	1	Jackman, JJB.	51
Cairns,GA.	66	French, JA.	228	Jackson, NC.	4
Cameron, D.	1	Furness, C.	41	Jamieson, DA.	57
Campbell, JC.	34	Gaje Gale	106	Jefferson, FA.	54
Campbell, K.	4	Ganju Lama	108	Kamal Ram	150
Campbell, L. MacL.	102	Gardner, PJ.	28	Karamjeet Singh Judge	160
Chapman, ET.	78	Garland, DE.	4	Kelliher, R.	228
Charlton,EC.	40	Gian Singh	160	Kenna, E.	228
Cheshire, GL.	4	Gibson, GP.	4	Kenneally, JP.	40
Chhelu Ram	149	Gordon, JH.	228	Keyes, GCT.	8
Chowne, A.	228	Gould, TW.	1	Kibby, WH.	228
Clarke, WAS.	90	Gratwick, PE.	228	Kingsbury, BS.	228
Cosens, A.	216	Gray, RH.	207	Knowland, GA.	57
Cruickshank, JA.	4	Gray, T.	4	Lachhiman Gurung	109
Cumming, AE.	156	Grayburn, JH.	103	Lalbahadur Thapa	104
Currie,DV.	213	Gristock, G.	57	Lassen, AFEVS.	115
Cutler, AR.	221	Gunn, GW.	34	Leakey, NG.	204
Derrick, TC.	228	Gurney, AS.	228	Learoyd, BAB.	4
Donnini, D.	74	Hannah, J.	4	Lee, BAW. W-	1
Durrant, TF.	36	Harden, HE.	131	Le Patourel, HW.	92
Eardley, CM.	69	Harman, JP.	46	Liddell, IQ.	38
Edmondson, JH.	228	Harper, JW.	98	Lifton, JW.	1
Edwards, HI.	4	Hinton, JD.	234	Lord, DSA.	4
Elliott, K.	234	Hoey, CF.	59	Lyell, The Lord,	39
Esmonde, EK.	3	Hollis, SE.	73	Mackay, JB.	228
Fazal Din	153	Hornell, DE.	208	Magennis, JJ.	1

Mahoney, JK.	216	Prakash Singh	157	Sukanaivalu, S.	235
Malcolm, HG.	4	Premindra Singh Bhagat	36	Swales, E.	188
Manser, LT.	4	Queripel, LE.	47	Thaman Gurung	106
Mantle, JF.	1	Ram Sarup Singh	143	Thompson, G.	4
Merritt, CCI.	216	Randle, JN.	57	Tilston, FA.	216
Middleton, RH.	220	Rattey, RR.	228	Topham, FG.	216
Miers, ACC.	1	Raymond, C.	36	Trent, LH.	230
Mitchell, GA.	122	Reid, W.	4	Trigg, LA.	230
Mynarski, AC.	208	Richhpal Ram	149	Triquet, P.	216
Namdeo Jadhao	148	Roberts, PSW.	1	Tulbahadur Pun	107
Nand Singh	155	Rogers, MAW.	97	Turner, HV.	71
Netrabahadur Thapa	106	Roope, GB.	1	Turner, VB.	114
Nettleton, JD.	4	Ryder, PED.	1	Umrao Singh	34
Newman, AC.	62	Savage, WA.	1	Upham, CH. + bar	234
Newton, WE.	220	Scarf, ASK.	4	Wakeford, R.	92
Ngarimu, M.N-a-K	234	Seagrim, DA.	73	Wakenshaw, AH.	70
Nicholls, H.	37	Sephton, AE.	1	Wanklyn, MD.	1
Nicholson, EJB.	4	Sherbahadur Thapa	110	Ward, JA.	230
Norton, GR.	206	Sherbrooke, R. StV.	1	Watkins, T.	79
Osborne, JR.	216	Sher Shah	161	Weston, WB.	73
Palmer, RAM.	4	Sidney, WP.	37	Wilkinson, T.	1
Parkash Singh	150	Smith, EA.	216	Wilson,ECT.	44
Partridge, FJ.	228	Smythe, QGM.	205	Wright, PH.	38
Peters, FT.	1	Stannard, RB.	1	Yeshwant Ghadge	148
Place, BCG.	1	Starcevich, LT.	228		
Porteous, PA.	34	Stokes, J.	69		

Others (Post-Great War)

Andrews, HJ.	182
Badcoe, PJ.	229
Carne, JP.	85
Curtis, PKE.	67
Henderson, GS.	56
Ishar Singh	167
Jones, H.	103
Kenny, WD.	169
McKay, IJ.	103
Meynell, G.	156
Muir, K.	102
Payne, K.	229
Rambahadur Limbu	111
Simpson, RS.	229
Speakman, W.	95
Wheatley, KA.	229
The Unknown Warrior of the U.S.A.	236

BIBLIOGRAPHY

The Victoria Cross Citations. *The London Gazette.*

The Author's Victoria Cross Files. James W. Bancroft.

The V.C. and D.S.O. (Vol. 1). Sir O'Moore Creagh VC. and E.M. Humphris.

The Lummis Files. The National Army Museum.

The Victoria Cross. Lt-Col. Rupert Stewart, M.V.O.

The Register Of The Victoria Cross. This England Books.

The Victoria Cross At Sea. John Winton.

For Valour: The Air VC's. C. Bowyer.

The Story Of The Victoria Cross 1856-1963. Sir John Smyth.

NOTES